iPod, Therefore I Am

By the Same Author

Jim Morrison: Dark Star

iPod,

Therefore I Am

Thinking Inside the White Box

Dylan Jones

BLOOMSBURY

Published by Bloomsbury Publishing,
New York and London
Distributed to the trade by Holtzbrinck Publishers

All papers used by Bloomsbury Publishing are natural, recyclable products
made from wood grown in well-managed forests. The manufacturing
processes conform to the environmental regulations of the country of origin.

Library of Congress Cataloging-in-Publication Data

Jones, Dylan, 1960–
    iPod, therefore I am: thinking inside the white box / Dylan Jones.—1st U.S.
ed.
    p. cm.
    ISBN-10: 1-59691-021-6 (hardcover)
    ISBN-13: 978-1-59691-021-8 (hardcover)
    1. iPod (Digital music player).   I. Title.

    ML74.4.I48J66 2005
    780'.285'65—dc22

                                                        2005006309

First U.S. Edition 2005

1   3   5   7   9   10   8   6   4   2

Typeset by Westchester Book Group
Printed in the United States of America
by Quebecor World Fairfield

Contents

There are other things in life besides music. I forget what they are, but they're around.

Hoagy Carmichael, composer of "Stardust" and "Georgia on My Mind"

Introduction

I Am a Jukebox

"My name is Dylan Jones and I am addicted to music . . ."

My transparent Macally mouse glows red as my index finger clicks left. I'm opening iTunes on the vertical panel bar, slipping into my library, a library that currently contains 4,399 songs (enough for 12.2 days of continuous music, taking up 29.96 GB).

I open a jewel case and slip the CD into the disc port in my PowerBook G4. Seconds later an icon appears on my desktop, half an inch in diameter, a fairly accurate approximation of a disc: Audio CD, it says (although it really looks like an old-fashioned vinyl disc in miniature); I'm at home and have not dialed-up—broadband is some weeks away as BT struggles to reach détente between my modem and its phone lines.

The track listing springs up on my screen, fifteen songs, all Beatles covers. One of two free CDs given away with *Mojo* magazine, this is *Beatlemania/Volume 1*, and I'm about to upload the Cyrkle's rather inspired, slightly odd, and deliberately out-of-tune version of "I'm Happy Just to Dance with You," the Lennon and McCartney song originally from

A Hard Day's Night (I think it's inspired and odd because it changes key when you least expect it, underscoring my theory that all really exceptional songs change key when you least expect them to).

I highlight the song with the bright blue horizontal four-millimeter-deep band, drag it across into the library, and then gaze through the window at the top of iTunes as it up-loads. It still feels magical, and watching the input bar fill up, I'm reminded of all those *Mission Impossible*–type films where a computer whiz tries to defuse a briefcase bomb before his laptop starts flashing "ABORTED." Fifteen seconds later, "I'm Happy" is nestling at the bottom of my library, waiting for me to punch in its details. And after I do, typing the album and song title first, so the song doesn't move before I've finished, it bounces up into its rightful alphabetical place, track no. 4,400, ready and waiting, and now very much part of my life. I go and look for it—why, I don't know, as it's always going to be there, unless I get tired of it and delete it—and of course there it is, nestling quietly, quite properly, between "Move on Up" by Curtis Mayfield and "You're the One for Me" by D Train.

And so I double-click on it and play.

And then I go wandering, scrolling up and down the library, looking for songs the way I once flicked through albums in record shops back when I was twelve, flicking through for no other reason than to convince myself they are still there. As I scroll, I find something I thought I'd deleted—fantastic!—a Groove Armada song I no longer like. More room for something else, more gigabites for the CDs I'm going to buy tomorrow, for the Rufus Wainwright song I'm going to download from iTunes ("Rebel Prince" from *Poses*). I press the right-hand side of my mouse and scroll down to Clear, and after my PowerBook asks me twice if I really, *seriously* want to delete the song not only from my playlist but also from my library, it is gone, banished to that ungodly place where unwanted MP3 files presumably go to die. And having deleted it, I move on, move up, scroll down, wander around, and wallow in a lifetime's love and affection.

Every record I've ever owned and kept is on this machine, from Alice Cooper's "Elected" right up to Shapeshifters' happy house classic "Lola's Theme." One is a record I bought after seeing it performed on *Top of the Pops*, the other after I heard it in an Ibizan nightclub. My whole life is here, 40 GB of memory, thirty years of memories. Every song I've ever cared about is in here somewhere, waiting in its spot hugging the wall until it's chosen to dance.

I feel as though I'm in a pinball machine or a computerized one-arm bandit, bouncing arbitrarily between 1950s doo-wop and 1990s alt-country, from the Delfonics to the Thorns via Creedence Clearwater Revival and the Pogues. I am a jukebox, and it feels good.

I open the cupboard in my den and take out my Power-Pod, the white lead that I use to connect the iPod with the G4. The connection is made, and the iPod begins uploading the new additions to the library, a further 154 songs. A few minutes later the exercise is completed, and my iPod is full—prone but proud. The iPod lies on the desk in front of me, looking a little like a speaker box. It is white, oblong, ergonomic, with perfectly rounded corners and a pale blue two-inch LCD window that lights up superbrightly for exactly two seconds when I touch one of its buttons (I have told it to do this and it does what it's told). It's made from this most remarkable plastic, a double-crystal polymer

Antarctica that looks like the most modern material ever invented.

The light recedes and then jumps back to life; it's winking at me, letting me know it's available and ready. It's willing and able, too, hinting that its vast library is there for the taking; all I need to do is press the Menu button and spin the wheel, scrolling down the songs to, let me see . . . how about "A Man Needs a Maid" by Neil Young, from *Harvest*, released during that period when he wanted to be James Taylor and I was trying to persuade my mum to buy me my first pair of flared jeans. My iPod tells me that this is the first song I'm playing from a possible 4,400 (I knew that!), and, right now as I'm typing, that it's 1:22 into the song with, 1:41, no, 1:33 left. How clever is that? This is a facility I never really thought about, a facility I never realized I wanted, or needed, but now of course can't live without. At least I don't think I can. But I feel that way about the iPod generally. The feelings I have toward my iPod (my intuitive little iPod), toward my G4, toward the Pod's iconic white headphones, toward everything associated with it are almost unnatural.

The iPod has consumed my life like few things before it. It sits in my office, daring me to play with it, like some sort of sex toy. As well as being the greatest invention since, oh, that round thing that cars tend to have four of, or those thin slivers of bread that come in cellophane packets, the iPod is also obviously a thing of beauty. And I think I'm beginning to really fall in love. Seriously . . .

Steve Jobs Changes His World

What you didn't know about the Apple CEO

Sometimes, critical mass happens when we least expect it. Early in 2004 Steve Jobs noticed something as he was walking through New York City. "I was on Madison," said the Apple CEO, "and it was, like, on every block, there was someone with white headphones, and I thought, 'Oh, my God, it's starting to happen.'" Bizarrely, Jonathan Ive, the company's sought-after style guru and the man behind the design of the iPod, had a similar experience in London: "On the streets and coming out of the Tube, you'd see people fiddling with it." By the summer of 2004 Apple had sold more than three million iPods to three million people for whom the little plastic and chrome computer with the capacious disc drive had become a way of life. It had sold them to Will Smith, Gwyneth Paltrow, Bill Clinton, Jamie Cullum, Sheryl Crow, Kevin Bacon, Public Enemy's Chuck D, Alanis Morissette, David Bowie, Ice T, Robbie Williams, and every other compressed, digitized celebrity worth his or her salt. The couturier Karl Lagerfeld bought himself sixty of the damn things, coded on their backs by laser etching so he could tell them apart (he even commissioned a pink copper rectangular purse to hold twelve at any one time). *Vanity Fair* editor Graydon Carter was given his by Steve Earle (who had already filled it with five thousand of his favorite songs). By April 2002 Apple's iPod had 51 percent of the digital music player market, with the remaining 49 percent being split with the Rio, RCA Lycra, iRiver, and Digital Way (digital music players you never, ever wanted to be seen with). By 2008 there will be eighteen million digital players in the world, and more than ten million of those will be iPods.

Suddenly, people were no longer listening to Walkmans—why would they, when they could carry their entire record collection around with them? Why limit yourself to sixty, ninety minutes of music when you could have forty thousand minutes on tap, at the turn of a wheel? Suddenly the iPod had galvanized a generation. In a Yahoo survey, a fifth of British backpackers said they wouldn't leave home without one. Although unlike previous musical revolutions, this was embraced by a much wider demographic, a demographic that had *(a)* access to a computer, *(b)* the means to buy a digital music player, and *(c)* taste in music—any taste. The fans of the iPod were not just eighteen years old; they were twenty-five, thirty, forty-five, *sixty*. Owners consumed everything from Maroon 5 to Beethoven, from Nirvana to Pink Floyd. They listened to their little white machines on the bus, on the subway, on the train, in the bath. Everywhere. Almost overnight, the iPod became a private club with a membership of millions. And not only did people begin buying iPods, they started buying iPod accessories—often third-party accessories—with a frenzy not seen since the dot-com boom at the end of the last century (when all people were buying were shares in dreams): external speakers (Altec

Lansing in particular), microphones, leather carriers, plastic "skins," iTrip transmitters that amplified the iPod through a car stereo, even special adaptors to fit a BMW or Smart car, enabling people to play their iPods on the journey to work (or, if the inclination strikes, Shanghai . . .). It was the first gadget to really appeal to the fickle consumer as well as to the computer nerd. And everyone found a different use for it. Sure, you could store your entire collection of Bob Dylan albums on it (should any such thing be attractive to a person), but its vast storage space made it a useful vault for all manner of digital files: the makers of the *Lord of the Rings* films used iPods to transport dailies from the film set to the studio.

When Steve Jobs returned to the company he cofounded in 1997, there were no plans for a digital music player—far from it. But having failed to notice the impending explosion in digital music, he set about creating a piece of "jukebox" software soon to be known as iTunes.

The story of Apple is a convoluted one, but a story that nonetheless makes for easy reading. Having dropped out of university in Oregon in the early 1970s, the long-haired, sandal-wearing, teenage Jobs, who lived entirely on fruit, teamed up with school friend Steve Wozniak and, in true American dream fashion, invented the world's first bonafide personal computer in Jobs's stepfather's garage. The computer, he'd tell anyone who'd listen, was going to be the bicycle of the mind. When the two met, doing summer work at Hewlett-Packard, Wozniak was only eighteen, and Jobs just thirteen. Jobs was never an underachiever (How could he be? After all, he was born and raised in Palo Alto, California, soon to become Silicon Valley)—he was a believer.

To finance the company—Apple was named after his favorite fruit—Jobs sold his Volkswagen camper van and

Wozniak his treasured programmable computer, which raised $1,300. Weeks later, Jobs secured his first order of fifty Apple 1 computers. Semi-cased in timber and initially costing $666.66,[1] the original 1975 Apple is today enshrined in the Smithsonian Institution, where it looks so much older than it actually is (once compared to a component from a 1930s telephone exchange, it made a Mackintosh chair look positively high tech). Unreliable and bulky, it was not a great success, and so they started again, coming up with the Apple 11, not the world's first personal computer, but soon the most popular (plastic case, built-in keyboard, colored graphics, the lot). It defined low-end computers for decades to come, and it was said that twenty-third-century archaeologists excavating some ancient PC World stockroom would see no significant functional difference between an Apple 11 from 1978 and an IBM PS/2 from 1992.

Many schools found that buying a few Apples was a cheap way to add computing to their curriculum. Apple 11's breakthrough was an application called VisiCale, the first proper spreadsheet, released in 1979, when Jobs was twenty-four. Between 1978 and 1983, Apple sales grew by 150 per-

[1] While working at HP, Wozniak started a "business" called, without a hint of irony, Dial-a-Joke. Each morning he'd record a joke into his home answering machine, which people were then encouraged to call. At its peak, more than two thousand people called per day, making it one of the most dialed numbers in the Bay Area. Of course, Wozniak made no money from it, since no one at the time knew how to charge for such calls. Wozniak's Dial-a-Joke phone number was 255-6666. Repeating numbers appealed to Wozniak immensely, and when Jobs suggested a retail price of $650 for the Apple 1, Wozniak countered with $666, then eventually $666.66.

cent a year, but those sales were based on the home and education markets. Jobs realized that the big money to be made from desktop computing would come from the business world. Apple needed to get into offices; they needed a business computer. And so they launched the Apple iii. But, like the Apple i, it was a bomb—it ran hot and frequently crashed and was soon overtaken in sales by IBM's recently launched PC. It was 1981 and Apple didn't know what to do next.

Two years later Jobs called John Sculley, then at Pepsi, and asked him to become president of Apple. "If you stay at Pepsi, five years from now all you'll have accomplished is selling a lot more sugar water to kids," Jobs told him. "If you come to Apple, you can change the world." So Sculley joined, leaving Jobs to obsess about creating the perfect low-cost computer. Jobs devoted all his time to this project, while Sculley ran the company, which, he soon discovered, was an organizational mess (rivals referred to Apple's Cupertino, California, headquarters as "Camp Runamok"). Jobs had not only met his nemesis; he'd employed him, and given him the power to fire him. Which is exactly what Sculley did. Eventually, a frustrated Sculley concluded that the main reason for Apple's problems was Jobs's erratic management style, and so stripped him of his day-to-day responsibilities.

Jobs may have been erratic, but it was his passion that drove him on. By the early 1980s Apple had expanded to such an extent that its campus was scattered across more than a dozen buildings in Cupertino, buildings that were full of engineers, designers, technicians, marketers, publicists, couriers, most of whom dressed in the regulation Silicon Valley uniform of T-shirt, jeans, and sneakers. As everyone looked the same—how could you tell if there was an IBM or a Compaq spy in the house?—it was decided that ID badges should be introduced: Steve Wozniak was declared employee number 1, Steve Jobs was number 2, and so on. But Jobs didn't want to be number 2; in fact he didn't want to be number 2 in anything. And so he argued that it was he, and not Wozniak, who should be the sacred number 1 since they were cofounders of the company and *J* came before *W* in the alphabet. Childish, yes, but then this was what Jobs was like. When the plan was rejected, he argued that as the number 0 was unassigned, he'd be quite happy to have it. Which he did, and as 0 came before 1, he was technically top dog. It didn't matter that Wozniak was the chief technician and designer; Jobs had his number. "Steve Jobs created chaos because he would get an idea, start a project, then change his mind two or three times, until people were doing a kind of random walk, continually scrapping and starting over," says one insider. "Apple was confusing suppliers and wasting huge amounts of money doing initial manufacturing steps on products that never appeared."

In 1986 Sculley relieved Jobs of his chairmanship, ironically just eighteen months after Apple had launched its breakthrough product, the Macintosh, a computer with a built-in screen and a mouse-and-click user interface (and called Macintosh after the favorite apple variety of its designer, Jef Raskin). At last, computers were accessible to the average user, who no longer had to type in obscure demands to carry out simple tasks. They created screen icons, cleaned up the keyboard, and successfully demystified the computing process. Jobs, always a master of marketing, propelled sales with a TV ad, directed by Ridley Scott, featuring an athlete being chased by storm troopers past throngs of vacant-eyed workers and hurling a sledgehammer at a menacing Big Brother face staring out of a screen. The message was that 1984 would not be Orwell's but Apple's. Jobs said at the time, "We started out to get a computer in the hands of everyday people, and we succeeded beyond our wildest dreams." The Macintosh's technology was so advanced that the Pentagon banned all exports to the Soviet Union.

But Jobs was gone, a centimillionaire with no job. He'd been given his "fuck-you money" from Apple, he'd been on the cover of *Time*, he was a pop-culture icon for Chrissakes!—what was he going to do now? He pondered a few options: (1) He thought of asking NASA if he could fly on one of the space shuttles, maybe as soon as the following year on the *Challenger*, (2) he visited the Soviet Union with a view to selling school computers to Mikhail Gorbachev, (3) and, perhaps even more fancifully, he considered making a bid for a Senate seat in California. But then, after a bicycle trip through Tuscany, he decided to do something far more prosaic: he'd get together a few engineers and do it all over again—he'd launch another computer company. He called his software company NeXT ("the next big thing") and also bought a fledgling animation firm from *Star Wars* director George Lucas "that needed vision." That company was Pixar, these days the digital animation studio behind *Toy Story*, *Monsters Inc.*, *A Bug's Life*, *Finding Nemo*, and *The Incredibles*, films that between them have grossed more than three billion dollars.

He returned to Apple as "interim CEO" in 1997 at the request of a board desperate for innovation and, says Jobs, "to salvage its fortunes." Given that the company nearly folded in 1995, this isn't as cocky as it sounds, and Jobs soon made his mark by cleaning house, streamlining the product lines, and jumping on the Internet bandwagon. He quickly launched the brightly colored iMac desktop computers—a hit with every design-obsessive from Cupertino to Clerkenwell—and followed them with the PowerBook and the iBook laptops, the flat-screen iMac (with its fifteen-inch LCD monitor and G4 processor), the OS X upgrade Panther, and the PowerMac G5, arguably the fastest desktop computer on the planet. Jobs also made peace with Microsoft, adapting many of his operating systems to be compatible with its Windows product.

Always, Jobs was obsessed with design and presentation, obsessed with how a product felt and how a product looked, as much as with how it worked. If there's anything PC users should be thankful to Apple for, it's that their PCs probably aren't quite as ugly as they used to be. Jobs brought the computers' looks to the forefront and made PC manufacturers step back, take a look at the ugly beige and greige boxes on their desks, and try to create something a little more scintillating. As soon as he introduced the five colored iMacs at the tail end of the 1990s, suddenly all computers, all white goods, every toaster, vacuum cleaner, and CD player looked as though they had been sent to the ergonomic doctor (even Rolex introduced iMac-influenced watches with translucent plastic in pastel colors). Apple's design sensibility—which was driven almost exclusively by Jobs and Jonathan Ive— was now so much a part of the company's DNA that unless each new product line substantially improved upon its predecessor, it was considered a failure; the Zen-like simplicity of a product's functionality only worked in conjunction with the brutal simplicity of its design. And if the company didn't get it right, there was a small army of devotees to tell it so. The company subscribed to the inverse law that says supply generates its own demand. If Apple made stuff, people bought it. Apple had become a cult that rewarded the loner, a badge of honor you could wear in your own home. Own an iMac, an iBook, or a PowerMac and you could be king without even getting dressed. Steve Jobs had not only steered one of Silicon Valley's greatest companies to fame and fortune by creating some of the most sought-after products of the age, but he had also emancipated a generation of nerds.

But, successful and as innovative as he was, who could have known Jobs would take Apple into digital music?

I Came, iPod, I Conquered

How I fell in love with the iPod

The first time I saw one, I wanted to steal it. Martyn wouldn't mind, would he? He could jump on a plane back to L.A. and buy another one. This one—the one in my hand, smiling at me—was only a few weeks out of its box, having just recently endured the twelve-hour flight from California to London in Martyn's carry on. I felt a bit desperate and rather giddy (which is odd, because I was sitting down). It was small, smaller than a cigarette packet, a white and chrome little thing measuring 2.43 inches wide by 4.02 inches tall by 0.78 of an inch thick. Its serial number was laser-etched on the back in the smallest, daintiest typeface, instead of being printed on a tacky-looking sticker. It was quite heavy, but not too heavy. It felt good in my hand, like some sort of squashed mobile phone. A squashed mobile phone that had shrunk my friend's record collection ("Honey, I shrunk my record collection!"), turning every musical moment of his life, every adolescent memory, every chorus of "Hi Ho Silver Lining," every last dance, every memorable car journey, into imperishable MP3 form. He'd only had it two weeks but had already squeezed several decades of his life into it, into this . . . this iPod.

It was the new one, the 3G, the one that would carry ten thousand songs, ten thousand MP3 files full of Pink Floyd, Kelis, Slaughter and the Dogs, anything he damn well liked. It had a tiny screen, like the sort you get on fancy mobiles—was he sure it wasn't a mobile?—four little buttons, and this lovely control wheel that seemed to do everything. I'd heard it described as the musical equivalent to Doctor Who's Tardis, and that's just what it was, a white plastic and chrome Tardis. It had this great "shuffle" facility that, when you pressed it, meant that the Roy Ayers track Martyn was playing could just as easily be followed by one by the Clash, Roberta Flack, Pilot, or the Fugees. Mad. It mixed up his music with, as he said, "the thoroughness of a blackjack dealer." Like I said, mad.

And the interface rocked: he could get to any song, artist, album, or playlist in under three seconds. Did I want one? What do you think? It was just lying there, daring me to fill it. All white, all new, all twenty-first century. Apple CEO Steve Jobs says he knows a machine is good if he wants to lick it, but with the iPod you might think about going a little bit further.

Could the iPod have come at a better time? I have been buying records, tapes, and CDs for thirty years, a journey that began with my mum and dad's seven-inch singles before kick-starting proper with *Middle of the Road's Greatest Hits* ("Soley Soley," "Chirpy Chirpy Cheep Cheep," "Twee-dle Dee Tweedle Dum," "Sacramento," etc.) and Alice Cooper's "Elected." A journey whose latest ports of call were two Libertines CDs, the Divine Comedy's "Absent Friends," and a rerelease of Jeff Buckley's *Grace*.

At home I have an entire wall of CDs, around ten feet of twelve-inches and vinyl albums, three boxes of singles, and approximately one hundred cassettes, mostly self-compiled (home taping didn't kill music in this house), kept in what looks like a purpose-built box that actually once housed a leopard-skin Dolce & Gabbana cushion (which I was given, before you ask). I've also got a shelfful of minidiscs, which rub up against the minidisc player my brother kindly gave me several Christmases ago. Having spent twenty years as a journalist, many of which have been spent listening to records professionally, I have acquired an astonishing amount of stuff that I wouldn't necessarily have bought but that has enriched my life immeasurably.

I also still spend a load of money on CDs, and not a week goes by without a random purchase or two. I have records I've played five hundred times or more (Stevie Wonder's *Songs in the Key of Life*, Steely Dan's *Aja*, and David Bowie's *Ziggy Stardust* for starters) and records I probably have not played all the way through. Records I bought and kept because they were trendy (UK Electro anyone? The The's *Infected*? *The Holy Bible*? Any Lou Reed record made after 1973?), records I refused to throw away for sentimental reasons but are, quite obviously, rubbish. And although I usually ignore my wife's repeated claims that I have too many records, she's right: I do. I probably have too many books and magazines too (I definitely have too many clothes), but having just moved, and having spent weeks putting records into boxes, records that I'm sure I hadn't looked at since the last time I took them out of a box, six years ago (the last time we moved), I thought maybe I should do something about it.

So I bought an iPod.

It's all Martyn's fault really, and in my mind I'm still sitting in his garden in West London, holding the damn thing in my hand, wondering if I could find enough time in my life to fill it up. And would I have enough time to use it? I have a job, a demanding job, and a wife and a family, and friends (honestly, I do), and a social life, and a pile of books by my bed that never seems to get any smaller, and a daily, weekly, monthly intake of newspapers, magazines, press releases, DVDs, CDs, book proofs, book catalogs, videos of forthcoming TV shows, bribes, blah, blah, blah. Then there were all the functions, the openings, the parties, the launches, and the nightly round of shaking the hand that feeds me. Add to this all the stuff on the Internet, the news bulletins, the e-mail correspondence, the Web site trawling, the this and the that and the whatever. I didn't have time to watch terrestrial television, so how was I going to fit an iPod into my life? "Seriously," said my friend John, "how much free time do you really have?"

None. Which is why I decided to buy an iPod. Or rather, I asked my wife to buy me one for Christmas, a Mac-compatible, 40 GB monster that would satisfy all my needs. Well, my wants anyway.

I already had the computer, a brand-spanking-new twelve-inch PowerBook G4 that was capable of burning CDs, in addition to having the intriguing iTunes logo in the vertical panel bar. iTunes would soon become my best friend, my first software buddy, the new home for my soon-to-be-shrinking record collection. I had bought the computer precisely for this reason: so my iPod would have somewhere to call home. I was slightly irritated that the MP3 generation seemed to be having more fun than I was, and having spent the best part of three decades collecting records, didn't see why I should be missing out. MP3s? Computers? Compressed files? I can do that.

My wife wrapped up the iPod just like she'd wrapped up last year's digital video camera and on Christmas morning, handed it over with a slight I-hope-you're-going-to-use-this-you-know-because-I-went-to-an-awful-lot-of-trouble-to-get-it-as-they're-practically-sold-out-over-here-and-it-wasn't-exactly-cheap-you-know look in her eye.

Well, I hadn't let her down with last year's gift—I have hours and hours of insane family expeditions—and I was determined to be as enthusiastic this year. I unpacked the beautiful black and white boxes, began fiddling about, plugged everything in, and then proceeded to plan the rest of my life.

I started filleting my record collection, ripping the guts out of my vinyl and uploading them onto iTunes. I began spending every available minute rummaging through every CD, record, single, and cassette, looking for songs worthy of my new baby's attention. On day two I discovered I had *Hunky Dory* not just on CD, but on cassette, and also on vinyl—three times! The original, a mid-1980s rerelease with extra tracks and a gatefold sleeve, and a limited-edition Japanese picture disc of unknown provenance. The album was one of Bowie's most formative, a cornerstone of early-1970s British singer-songwriting, but did I need five copies? The process of deciding what to upload involved listening to every song I'd ever bought. Some were imported immediately, but many more were forced to walk my PowerBook's metaphorical plank. Would I rip it into an MP3, or would I press Eject and spin the CD out of its slit?

I fell in love with the process immediately. As soon as a song was uploaded, either by importing a whole CD or by individually dragging it across to my library, the file just lay there, nameless, blameless. And so I would type in the artist's name, the song title, and the album it came from (as well as host of other categories), and then watch it flip into its rightful place. After having spent a few nights doing this, my friend Robin, who had already become well versed in the ways of the Pod, said I should upload while connected to the Internet because the program would then download the information for you. Fantastic! Isn't the Internet brilliant! My own private radio station was being compiled right before my eyes—all I had to do was upload the content.

As soon as I got busy with my new toy, experts popped up everywhere, those know-it-alls who had been in Podland for some time now. Was I going to start burning CDs, seventy minutes of personalized taste to give to friends and family? Was I going to move up a gear and burn my first MP3 CD, a full eight and a half hours of compressed digital fun? How was I doing with Smart Playlists? Was I making my own CD covers yet? Had I downloaded anything from Limewire?

This was all before me, as what I was really enjoying was editing my life. I had spent far too much of my life compiling cassettes of my favorite music, either for myself or for friends—120-minute juxtapositions of the cool and the corny: esoteric Springsteen or doo-wop compilations, the A–Z of Suede, Go-Go's greatest hits (actually this easily fit on a C-60—four Trouble Funk tracks and, er, not much else). In my late twenties I began a series of "One Louder" cassettes, in homage to Spinal Tap, reaching "Twenty-one Louder" before running out of steam, but there were plenty of others too: "Terminal 1970s Freeway Madness" (side 1: "Fast Lane," Side 2: "Slow Lane," you get the picture), "Disco Epiphany," "Disco Nirvana," "Now That's What I

Call R.E.M.," "100 Minutes of the Clash," "The Best Beach Boys Tape in the World," "Everything She Wants" (a load of Wham! for an ex-girlfriend), "Metal Leg" (a shed-load of Steely Dan for myself), "Aimee Mann +" (must have been a slow week), "Christ It's the Chemical Bros!" and "David Bowie."

Albums ceased to matter, and I could edit with impunity. Why bother with R.E.M.'s *New Adventures in Hi-Fi* when all you really want is "Electrolite" and "E-Bow the Letter"? Why continue to ruin *Pet Sounds*, the best album recorded by anyone in the 1960s, by suffering the absurdity of "Sloop John B" when you can simply delete it? Having embraced iTunes, I could now listen to the Beatles albums without any of the Ringo tracks. My version of the Clash's *Give 'Em Enough Rope* no longer included "Julie's Been Working for the Drug Squad," while "Stairway to Heaven" had miraculously vanished from my edition of *Led Zeppelin IV*. Shame. For me, iTunes became a great leveler, butting Thelonious Monk up against the Carpenters, Mylo up against Dusty Springfield, Oasis up against Elvis. I rediscovered the joys of Miles Davis and began questioning why I had ever liked Lenny Kravitz or drum 'n' bass. Abba? Check. The Cult? What had I seen in them in the first place (even though "She Sells Sanctuary" was still worthy of uploading)?

The iPod not only changed the way I felt about music; it helped me reestablish relationships with records I hadn't heard in five, ten, twenty years. Bad Company's "I Can't Get Enough of Your Love" became a constant companion, as did Ace's "How Long" and Cracker's "Low." Zero 7 became gods in my eyes, as did the Yellow Magic Orchestra, Brian Eno, Phoenix, Bob Seger, and the Bees. All of a sudden they were living in my house, along with dozens of other pop stars I hadn't had anything to do with for ages.

I kept at it, uploading as though tomorrow were going out of fashion (Mike Skinner?! Genius! Rip him now!). In four months I'd uploaded more than 4,000 songs, using up nearly half the memory of my 40 GB iPod, creating the sort of library that would frighten the life out of any BBC radio programmer. As I compiled my library, I'd play back my acquisitions on shuffle, moving from Sugar to Nancy Sinatra to Scott Walker and Ryan Adams via the Beastie Boys and Beck. Perverse, accidental, and idiosyncratic . . . I'd never listened to music this way before. (Choice is meant to make you anxious, but not if someone else is doing the choosing.) I began to think: Could I get my entire record collection onto this machine? Could I get an entire lifetime's experience into this little white rectangle? Could I compress a life's worth of CDs, tapes, records, singles, and minidiscs onto my Pod? Okay, I might not have many minidiscs, but they're my minidiscs. Surely I couldn't collect all the good stuff that had ever been recorded. Could I? Could I really? In one place? Really? Could I? Surely I couldn't . . .

I wasn't consuming music so much as curating it, and the iPod had brought out the nerd in me; I was becoming an organizer, an alphabetizer. But then that was the point, I thought to myself. As I began compiling the library, as I worked my way through the hundreds of jewel cases in my den, the thought occurred to me that I shouldn't just turn my machine into a virtual greatest-hits collection. There would be nothing clever about including every great Oasis track, every great Who song, or the complete works of Marvin Gaye. Anybody could do that, so why would that make my iPod special? It wouldn't, would it? And so the editing process became even harder: how could I upload my record collection without missing out the obvious bits but while also making it interesting, making it an artifact in its own right. If all the iPod did was collect all your stuff in one place, then I could simply ask someone else to upload it for me, and where would be the fun in that? I may as well have gone to one of those companies—a growth industry this—who compile bespoke iPods for you . . . 15 GB, 20 GB, 40 GB, you name it. Or else I could ask them to fill one with stuff they thought I might like, making it a different sort of consumer purchase completely. The big thing about the iPod, I thought, was the way in which it forces you to listen to your life in a different way. If I had wanted someone else's juxtaposition to accompany me on airplanes and taxi rides, then I could have started doing that when I was fourteen and simply asked other people to buy my records for me. No, I had to put more effort into this. I had to begin to take it seriously.

And so the editing began in earnest. While I was uploading Air's *Moon Safari*, an album I thought I needed in its entirety, I started thinking I might not need all of it, which forced me to go back in and find out if this were true. And as for *Talkie Walkie*, their follow-up, after repeated plays it turned out I only really liked three songs, "Universal Traveler," "Alpha Beta Gaga," and "Alone in Kyoto" (and none of them are exactly crucial). And as for the canon, well, it just wasn't going to work. There are many so-called classic albums that I have never particularly seen the point of, and when I started filling my iPod I realized I had been too lenient with them. *Electric Ladyland*? Two tracks, tops. *The*

Stone Roses? Five tracks, and that's pushing it. *Exile on Main Street*? I know it's always voted the best Stones album by critics and consumers alike, but it's got six decent songs, max. *Nevermind*? Nothing at all, thank you very much (Kurt Cobain wasn't a spokesman for my generation, and I hope he hasn't remained a spokesman for anyone else's). Same goes for *Pearl* by Janis Joplin, a singer almost as untalented and as physically repellent as Shaun Ryder. My iPod didn't care a fig for the canon, and it wasn't going to start liking records just because it ought to, just because *Rolling Stone* and *Q* and *Mojo* said it ought to. God knows I did enough of that. How many hours, days, weeks probably, did I waste as a teenager trying to like Emerson, Lake, and Palmer's *Pictures at an Exhibition* or Pere Ubu's "difficult" second album? Why did I bother pretending to like Black Uhuru? I was never going to like them, no matter how many times the *NME* told me I ought to. When you're filling up your toy, the only records you should concentrate on are the ones you love.

Anyway, I had my own canon, one built on experiences I had when I was back in my teens, when, if I chose to, I would play an album until I liked it, no matter how insubstantial it was. I'm sure this is why I still love *Ooh La La* by the Faces, a record the band not only struggled to finish (it doesn't even last thirty minutes) but was also disowned by Rod Stewart before the thing was even released (as he didn't bother turning up to the studio, the title track was eventually sung by Ron Wood). Because of my misplaced diligence I also have an unreasonable penchant for *Billion Dollar Babies* and *Muscle of Love* by Alice Cooper as well as *It'll Shine When It Shines* by the Ozark Mountain Daredevils—I'm fairly certain the record isn't any good but I've loved it for thirty years and will probably love it until I die. (I was fourteen, for Chrissakes, forgive me!)

Not only this, but a lot of stuff has simply been ruined by repetition and overexposure. In my student days I used to love Motown—the classics, the rarer-than-hen's-teeth B-sides, all of it—but now can hardly bear to listen to it. I played it so much in my youth, even played drums in a group that used to regularly butcher "Dancing in the Street," "Nowhere to Run," and "Heatwave," that by the time the advertising industry caught up with it in the mid-1980s, using Marvin Gaye and the Supremes to sell jeans and T-shirts, for me it was already past its sell-by date. How much Motown did I upload? Six songs, none of which are indispensable: "There's a Ghost in My House" by R. Dean Taylor, some Diana Ross, "It's a Shame" by the Spinners (the semiclassic single they made before moving to Atlantic), and a couple of things by the Four Tops. I've got more Robbie Williams than I have Motown, which, I like to think, makes me feel more modern than I actually am. I also refused to appreciate the blues, something I've done since seeing B. B. King on *The Old Grey Whistle Test* aged twelve. The blues are too depressing, too authentic, too rootsy for me, and the iPod wasn't going to change my mind.

I soon realized that the iPod is uniquely egalitarian, and in its eyes, especially through the prism of the shuffle facility, Alessi's "Oh Lori," Nick Heyward's "Whistle down the Wind," and Brian Protheroe's "Pinball" are equally as important as Led Zep's "Immigrant Song," Primal Scream's "Loaded," and the Fab Four's "Hey Jude." The shuffle facility became my own private energy source, my own electricity, running my life, accompanying my every move, choosing every song in my head. I'd chosen every song it played, I just hadn't told it when I wanted to hear it. Oh lordy. The shuffle meant my iPod could cut from Roland Kirk's "Fly by Night" to Ce Ce Peniston's "Finally"—as it did just now—as though it were the most natural thing in the world. I would never have made that choice, and I probably never will again, but my little chrome friend says it's perfectly okay. Algorithms gone crazy? You said it, guvnor.

Am I a better person? Well, I'm certainly a different person, an evangelist almost, for the pleasures of the chrome. Where once I was snotty and standoffish, I am now quite, quite devout. Ask me anything about the iPod and I will bore the pants off you. Ask me about "My Top Rated" and "Recently Played" or the pleasures of Smart Playlists and I won't shut up until you shove my iPod in my mouth. I have become someone to avoid at parties (even more so than usual), someone who can't be trusted with technical information. Why? Because I'm bound to retain it and pass it on. I might tell someone, and if you're unlucky it might be you. I am the iBore, the man who bought into Steve Jobs's dream as though it were his own, which in many ways it was. An obsession I have had since adolescence has been rekindled to the point where it's eating into my leisure time with Pacman-like intensity. I am not only beholden to a computerized jukebox no bigger than a mobile phone, but my expectations of it are also exponential. The iPod is a bottomless well, a black hole of limitless dimensions, a hobby that knows no bounds. As a fellow devotee said after he'd passed his own initiation ceremony—which lasted for about the same time as mine, approximately six months—"The role of the records themselves changes when you go digital. They shrink into the background. Your records and CDs were once the main event; now, in computer parlance, they are your backup, standing ready in case of catastrophic failure of your digital library. They're what you read while you listen and wait for a box big enough to store every song ever recorded."

So, have I changed? Maybe, like John Lennon said, "forever, not for better."

What I knew for sure was that I was hooked.

3

The Single: Seven Inches of Aural Sex

Teenage dreams, so hard to beat

I wish I could say that the first single I bought wasn't Gary Glitter's "I Didn't Know I Loved You (Till I Saw You Rock & Roll)." I wish it had been David Bowie's "Starman" (I already had that on cassette, having taped it from the radio, which doesn't really count), or Mott the Hoople's "All the Young Dudes" (a much, much better record that someone had already lent me, so I didn't really feel like buying it). Even the previous Gary Glitter record—"Rock & Roll, Part 1"—would have been better, cooler (at the time, anyway), but there you are. When you're twelve, you don't make history; you're just a victim of it. Still, as I bought it, handing over my hard-saved money, I felt as though I were moving from boyhood to adulthood, leaving shin pads and Cub Scouts behind, and embracing a world full of platform boots and chinchilla coats. The record sounded dangerous, Neanderthal, rough . . . big boy stuff.

Before the CD—*well* before the CD—and just after shellac and the 78, came the seven-inch single, the greatest form of teenage expression since premarital sex. The seven-inch single helped invent the notion of the teenager, and helped the 1960s prepare itself for some extreme social mobility. And I, like every other twelve-year-old boy I knew in 1973, was an extremely willing victim.

As a boy, singles were my life—they were what I lived for, what I spent my pocket money on. I couldn't afford many LPs, but singles could be bought every week.[2] At school, every break time was spent discussing what was going to be number one that week, and what singles we were going to buy on the weekend. Slade. Wizzard. Bowie. At that age, with puberty a constant companion, and inarticulacy a foregone conclusion, these records were how I spoke to the world. Largely I chose records that made the most noise, that had the most attitude, records that had the most pent-up emotion—Cockney Rebel, Bowie, Roxy, Golden Earring. Alice Cooper's "Elected," for instance, was so full of provocation that I felt my whole life was being expressed by it: it only lasted a couple of minutes, yet simply listening to it made me feel a little like I was performing myself—acting out my tortured internal world in one, 150-second, one-act play.

But I liked a lot of other stuff too. When I was young, I was fairly indiscriminate about the records I bought; I bought them because I liked them, not because they were cool or fitted into a particular adolescent agenda. It seems ridiculous now, when the world is remixed every five minutes

[2]My first LP purchase was Alice Cooper's *Billion Dollar Babies*, which I bought two weeks after it came out, in a small record shop in Deal, on the South Coast, paying for it in four weekly fifty-pence installments. I've also got a fairly strong recollection of paying £2.11 for *Dark Side of the Moon*, from Chiltern Sounds in Marlow, about a year after it was released.

to the sound of a recently acquired and no doubt soon-to-be-banished backbeat (could be garage, could be jungle, could be a garage in a jungle), but back in the early seventies people tended to either like long-haired white music or satin-swathed soul music. You went to gigs or went to discos. Liked the Who or Funkadelic, drank snakebite or cocktails. Me, I tended to like anything. In the first three years I spent buying records, from 1972 to 1975, I bought *everything*: glam rock, soul, disco, funk, heavy metal, folk, pub rock, the lot (I even had a David Cassidy single, "I Am a Clown," on the silver Bell label; in fact I've still got it). This was a period when an Acker Bilk record was as important to me as a Queen 45. I was falling in love with music, pure and simple, and while I knew I could easily be swayed by style, there were things I liked simply because I heard them on the radio. Who knew what Medicine Head looked like? I liked "One and One Is One" anyway. And did it matter that Lieutenant Pigeon were fronted by a pub pianist who looked like Dick Emery in drag? Like Bob Dylan once said about the Judy Garland song "The Man That Got Away," "This song always did something to me, not in any stupefying, tremendous kind of way. It didn't summon up any strange thoughts. It was just nice to hear."

We pick up music by osmosis when we're young, but we're also the victims of indoctrination. There was always music in my house, always Frank Sinatra and Dean Martin records on the gramophone, always the Beatles on the radio. The first film I ever saw was *A Hard Day's Night*, which my mother dutifully took me to when I was just four. She was also a brilliant pianist, and whenever she found time—usually on a Sunday—she would work her way through old music hall standards, wartime ballads, and "current songs from the hit parade" (as they said on the "wireless" at the time). One of the many things she used to play for me when I was young was a maudlin standard called "So Deep Is the Night," which had been adapted from an old Chopin piece (as opposed to a recent Chopin piece, that is). I'd heard it accompany one of the many TV compilations of classic silent-movie scenes that always seemed to be playing on Saturday mornings, and asked Mum if she could play it; she picked it up in less than five minutes.

My father also indoctrinated me by turning me on to Lou Reed, and specifically "Walk on the Wild Side," which he thought was tantalizingly decadent. These days it's played regularly on Radio 2, but back in 1972 it was about as risqué as a record could be and still be commercially successful. My father always tried to push me, always wanted me to exploit my intellect, which is probably why he got so frustrated when I didn't come up to scratch.

Why did I fall in love with music so much? Why does any twelve-year-old boy fall in love with pop? It's predestined, in a weird kind of way, like it is for everyone. With me, maybe it was because music would have me, because it made it so obvious it wanted to fall in love with me . . . *me*! And at the time, I felt I needed something, someone, quite badly.

If asked to identify the one thing that has caused me the most hardship in my life, the one vexation that has brought me most grief, I would have to point, not to a debilitating illness or handicap, but to the consonant that follows *ABC*.

D, how I hate you.

Of course *B*s, *G*s, and *S*s have occasionally wrecked havoc too, but it is the *D*s that have kept me awake at night, made me weak from anxiety and affected the way in which I see and talk to the world.

Stammering is not a particularly dignified affliction, tied in as it is with foppish dilettantes who wander around Waugh and Wodehouse novels like accidents waiting to happen. Stammerers are portrayed as crooks, perverts, idiotic chinless wonders, maladjusted members of the underclass, or, more usually, simply figures of fun: Michael Palin in *A Fish Called Wanda*, Ronnie Barker in *Open All Hours*. It is an affliction that rarely inspires anything but pity, or sarcasm. There is little solace in knowing that Marilyn Monroe had a discernible stammer; she also, apparently, had appalling BO. No one likes to stammer. It has no kudos. It is the aural equivalent of being clumsy, disconnected, uncoordinated: the involuntary repetition of mistakes. A stammer never goes away. It can disappear for a while, and it's easy to think it's gone for good. Then, all of a sudden, it's back, worse than before, a malevolent quirk that refuses to make life any easier.

A stammer (for what it's worth, *stammer* is still more desirable a word than *stutter*, though they mean exactly the same thing) is like a rash that invades your body at times of stress, a signal to the perpetually beleaguered that God hasn't quite forgotten, not just yet, anyway.

About one person in every hundred stammers, and it affects four times as many men as women. There is a 20 percent greater chance of you stammering if a close relative has a speech problem, although the roots almost always lie in childhood. Stammerers often have some difficulty learning words at a very young age, and emotional and physical stress on a child plays a big part. Some kids begin stammering to draw attention to themselves and then find they can't stop, although the attention is usually of the wrong kind.

My stammer was largely caused by my father, something

he now obviously—profoundly—regrets. It haunts him, or so my mother says. And though I believe him, and bear him no malice (I still love him), it haunted me too, for ages (my upbringing was so brilliant in so many other ways, but no one likes being hit, and no one likes being hit when they're young, particularly when they're very young). The way I was treated as a small boy scared me off fatherhood for years (it took me that time to realize that I didn't necessarily have to repeat my father's bad habits). Nowadays I think my relationship with my father is better than it's ever been, and because of our shared history I think we've both been extra careful with each other, and maybe know each other a bit better than we might have if things had been different. And in certain ways my stammer has defined me, made me what I am, whether I like it or not. Heigh-ho.

I have stammered since I was about five, and it was at school where it caused the most hurt, obviously. Children are remarkably resourceful when it comes to identifying someone's weak points, but with a stammer the ammunition is handed to them on a plate; with a stammer you are putting the bullets into their hands yourself. I don't remember much from those days, but I remember enough. Few things are more worrying when you're young than standing in the middle of a playing field with twenty other boys waiting to call out their names, knowing that when your turn comes, your stammer is only going to be exacerbated by the anxiety of getting it right. I also remember standing in the dinner queue, knowing that I was going to have immense difficulty asking for whatever was on the menu that day, the pressure increasing second by second as my school friends swiftly barked their requests before turning away.

Unless you've experienced it yourself, it's difficult to

imagine the abject depression of worrying about every single word that comes out of your mouth. Between the ages of about five and sixteen it was utter hell. Every request had to be worked out in advance, every joke required a run-up (and God help you if you fell at the punch line).

The tribulations of teenage angst are bad enough without literally being tongue-tied. Some women say they find a stammer attractive, an indication of sensitivity perhaps, or vulnerability. But no teenage girl ever finds a stammer attractive, at least not the ones I knew at thirteen.

Consequently, in my early teens, I started to become scared of speaking. At home I buried myself in my record collection, poring over my singles night after night, counting them just to make sure they were still there. I studied every nuance, every crackle, every scratch. Listening to songs on the radio or records at other people's houses was never the same, as they didn't have the same jumps and skips (I knew my records so well that I once identified David Bowie's "Rebel Rebel" from the run-in groove, before the riff came in).

Pulling myself away from my classmates, distancing myself from reality, I would while away the hours at school carrying on entire conversations in my head. I became monosyllabic, as grunting was easier than trying to say something that involved words, sentences, punctuation, opinion, thought, feeling, anything. I gravitated toward words I knew well—or at least words I was able to pronounce. In another attempt at self-defence, I forced my middle-class accent "downward": a little curt, more working class, blunt. If I sounded rougher than I looked, then maybe people would leave me alone, stop laughing at me or looking at me twice. My downwardly mobile accent worked to a certain extent, and soon my voice was indistinguishable from any other fourteen-year-old boy with a Home Counties lilt.

As I matured, I began taking my stammering for granted, and it became almost an integral part of my makeup. During my late-teenage years, when a different youth cult seemed to invade my life every six months or so, my stammer became a badge of notoriety, a symbol—like an earring or a black leather jacket—of a certain type of "otherness." But then I really did grow up, and the stammer (or at least its importance) faded from my life like so many Buzzcocks records. It was never completely debilitating, but seeing that my main hindrance was always the dreaded *D*, obviously one of the worst things for me had been announcing myself on the telephone. It had almost made me reluctant to introduce myself, which, as a journalist, caused all-too-palpable problems. I mastered it, though, and even grew to conquer public speaking, something I used to abhor.

But at age fourteen, I opted out of society and threw myself into my music, taking solace in my record collection. Safe in my room, a small upstairs room in a quarter at the top of a hill on an RAF base just outside London (I had seriously peripatetic parents), my sense of isolation was almost comforting I felt so removed. If adolescence is meant to be all about joining in—trends, gangs, clubs—I was in my own tree, all alone and quite content. For me and my friends, it wasn't the *idea* of music that brought us together, it was the way music made us feel (and this we didn't particularly articulate to each other). If you could listen to the opening bars of "Jean Genie" or "All the Way from Memphis" without getting a whiff of immortality, then there was obviously no hope for you. In those days I could sit and pour over a single as though it were a rare book, money, or pornography (which was extremely difficult to find then). A few years later I remember staring at a copy of the Damned's "New Rose" (Britain's first punk single, released at the end of 1976 on Stiff Records) as though it had some secret powers, and all I had to do to liberate those powers was to stare at it for hours on end. I stared at the damn thing as though it were a dead dog, fascinated and transfixed in equal measure.

I've still got some singles, 562 in all—some I've had all my life (they belonged to my parents), some since my teens, and a few I've even bought fairly recently. Many, like the first Public Image single (that came with its own spoof newspaper, designed by Terry Jones eighteen months before he launched i-D), ATV's "Love Lies Limp" flexidisc, and an original copy of the Who's "Substitute" are sheathed in clear-plastic covers. Some of my boyhood teenage singles have covers kept together by gaffer tape, Sellotape, masking tape, glue . . . Some are marked up with biro and felt-tip, tiny little telltale signs of my past. Every fold and crease is a memory, every tear and scratch. I've even got a copy of "Dishevelment Blues" by the Faces, which was given away with the NME in 1973. When the album Ooh La La was released, the paper gave out a free flexidisc as a promotional tool. The NME put five tracks from the album on side 1 and asked the band if they'd record something special for side 2. I found out thirty years later that they deliberately recorded an "abomination" in the hope that the paper wouldn't have the balls to use it. But the NME did, and I loved it. Love it still.

There are not just my memories in my singles collection, either, there are the semi-remembered memories of other people, the previous owners of my secondhand records, the ones with their names and obsessions felt-tipped on the covers. Who was "Sally," who drew her name in bubble writing on the cover of my copy of "Space Oddity"? Whose Rotring pen carved the harlequin shapes on the cover of "It's Different for Girls"?

These days I don't even look at sleeves—they're too small, and my life is too full. I've played Coldplay's *Parachutes* more than one hundred times, but if you held a gun to my head and asked me what is on the cover—an unlikely scenario, I admit, but you get my drift—I'm not sure I would be able to tell you. It's some sort of yellow circle, a sunlike sphere sitting on a black bed of Spinal Tap–type intensity. But back then, between the ages of twelve and eighteen, I knew everything about my singles: what was on the B-side, whether there was a note of its length, the color and provenance of the label, whether it was a rerelease (never a good thing), and—during punk—whether there was anything scratched into the run-out groove. I've still got all my Bowie singles—thirty-two total—all my T. Rex, all my Donna Summer, all my Buzzcocks . . . and dozens of Elvis Costello singles. I've got John Handy's "Hard Work" (Impulse, 1976), the Brothers Johnson's "Stomp" (A&M, 1980, picture sleeve), the Fall's "Bingo-Master's Break-Out!" (Step Forward, 1977, picture sleeve), Larry Wallis's "Police Car," still in its original Stiff sleeve, complete with two—count 'em!—catch phrases: "Today's sound today" and "If it means everything to everyone it must be a Stiff."

The 45-rpm single was introduced by RCA Victor in America on March 31, 1949, and lasted forty years before being replaced by the compact disc. It started life as a replacement for the shellac 78s, which had just been superseded by Columbia Records' latest invention, the 33⅓ LP. But as everyone preferred the Columbia version for "longer programming," the 45 became the standard for singles. The speed was based on calculations that proved that the best compromise between adequate signal-to-noise ratio and playing time was three minutes per radial inch (and not, as has become myth, that a spiteful RCA executive simply arbitrarily subtracted 33 from 78). According to the National Sound Archive, "Calculus was used to show that the optimum use of a disc of constant rotational speed occurs when the innermost recorded diameter is half the outermost recorded diameter." Which is why a seven-inch single has a label that's three and a half inches in diameter. It took seven years for 78s to completely die out, but by 1956, and the dawn of Elvis, of rock 'n' roll itself, the 45 had the market monopolized. That year, Columbia—RCA's "speed war" nemesis—developed car stereos that played custom-built 16-rpm discs with forty-five minutes of music pressed onto each side. RCA responded with a 45-rpm version, but who wanted to change singles every three minutes in the fast lane?

In the hodgepodge of my singles collection you will find many things (and a lot of it looks like it's been sandpapered within an inch of its life): Brook Benton's "Walk on the Wild Side," Culture Club's "I'm Afraid of Me," the first three Pigbag singles, Run DMC's "Walk This Way," the Edgar Winter Group's "Frankenstein," Marianne Faithfull's "As Tears Go By" ("I want a song with brick walls all around it, high windows, and no sex," said Rolling Stones manager Andrew Loog Oldham when he commissioned Jagger and Richards to write it for her), Oas*s's "Wibbling Rivalry" (the 1995 recording of Noel and Liam Gallagher fucking arguing with each other), the Human League's "The Sound of the Crowd," Boz Scaggs's "What Can I Say," Sly & the Family Stone's "Life," War's "Low Rider," that annoying Peter Frampton vocoder record ("Everybody in the world had

Frampton Comes Alive," says Wayne in *Wayne's World*. "If you lived in the suburbs, you were issued it. It came in the mail with samples of Tide"), Crowded House's "Don't Dream It's Over," Elvis Costello's "Alison" ("Forty year old stereo," it says on the A-side!), and Thomas Leer's "International" (a record that was, is, like the old Bob Dylan saying, "Cool as pie, hip from head to toe") . . . And because I am as much of a completist and a fetishist as the next man, there are my complete collections of Buzzcocks singles (punk brought back picture sleeves with a vengeance), T. Rex singles, Clash singles, Madness singles, Specials singles, all of them lovingly collated and neatly filed. Lovely.

For years I thought all I needed to compartmentalize my collection was a jukebox, although since I received the iPod I don't need one. The singles playlist I've been compiling is a soundtrack to my life, from 1972 to 1980, a soundtrack that can, in a flick of the wheel, conjure up any salient part of my youth. And if I flick to the right place, I'll land on David Bowie's "Rebel Rebel," as good an adolescent rallying cry as you're ever likely to hear, and a record that convinced me, at the tender age of thirteen, that life wasn't so bad after all. Who knows, I thought to myself, maybe this could be the life for me.

Maybe I could be a space face too.

4

A Glamour Profession

How Bryan Ferry and Roxy Music turned my head

At the age of twelve, cocooned in my room, in an attempt to create a respite from the domestic situation downstairs—there are signs that the incessant buzz of argument is going to ignite at any second—I am alone with my turntable, as I always am. It is about four years old, made in 1969 by Pye, a nondescript mass-market brand that never had Bang & Olufsen aspirations, and bought by my dad around the same time. It's flat and low and looks like one of those oo-scale models of new towns you used to see in civic centers in the early 1970s. Its plastic lid is smoked and folds down over the turntable with a reassuringly inaudible thump (it has strips of felt glued to its edges, which always make for a soft landing).

Even to my unnurtured mind I can tell it's a strange beast because when the cue arm finishes playing a record, instead of lifting itself up and returning to its seat, it simply follows the run-off groove to the center of the record, to the label, and then just dies, stops and lies there limp, as though the seismic notions contained within, say, Sly & the Family Stone's "Family Affair" or Dean Martin's "Volare" have caused it to collapse, exhausted by the emotional intensity of it all. When I was given the deck by my parents—I think they realized I needed solace and somewhere to go and play the odd-sounding records I was beginning to bring into the house and so bought themselves a state-of-the-art stereogram—and started mucking about with it, I began thinking they had just palmed it off on me because it was broken, but then I quite quickly realized that this was probably the greatest record player ever invented. Why? Because it meant that at night I could play a record while I was in bed and not have to worry about getting up and turning the damn thing off before I went to sleep. I could drift away listening to *The Man Who Sold the World* or *Dark Side of the Moon* or Bo Hansson's *Lord of the Rings* and imagine I was in the Wild West End of London or Middle-earth or indeed the dark side of the moon and not have to worry about coming home to switch off the stereo. I can tell you, at the age of twelve, it was tantamount to living in a case-study bachelor pad with sliding doors in the bathrooms, wall-mounted televisions in the bedroom, and wall-to-wall shag pile in the den.

But I'm not going to bed just yet as it's only eight-thirty. My seven-year-old brother is in bed next door and my mum and dad are still glowering silently at each other downstairs. It is a Saturday evening and they have just been watching *The Generation Game*. And I am alone, although not really. Like many a middle-class air force brat, having moved every eighteen months since I was born, my friends, my peers, are not like-minded twelve-year-olds, but rather circular pieces of black vinyl, seven and twelve inches in diameter, some of them with orange labels, some of them with purple, green, or yellow, but all of them as important to me as members of my immediate family. In fact, considering the fights that have been going on all week, a lot more important, and certainly a lot more consistent (they don't shout at me, and what they do say is always exactly, *exactly* the same). These records are my brothers and my sisters, the nieces and nephews I don't have. And I love them (not that I don't love my real brother, of course; it's just that he's not, you know, a record).

Last night it was Sinatra-esque dreamscapes of John Barry, Sergio Mendes, and Georgie Fame, although tonight I'm behaving like any twelve-year-old in 1973, playing the records of David Bowie, Alice Cooper, and T. Rex. Sure, I have become unduly fond of Dean Martin, Frank Sinatra, and the odd, possibly Scandinavian folk duo Nina and Frederick (the sort of polo-neck-wearing couple who in my naïveté I imagine enjoy threesomes and strong liquor rather than gimp masks and amyl nitrate), but on a purely visceral level I am obsessed by kohl eyeliner, Technicolor quiffs, space-age platform boots, and sloganeering glam rock.

Sixty-seven songs in my iPod library are largely the work of one man, Bryan Ferry, the Tyneside lounge lizard who, along with David Bowie and Marc Bolan, helped invent the 1970s. Right now—just now, as you're reading this—it's the future, but back then it was too. Mixing the glamour of nostalgia and edgy modernity is currently the order of the day, an unavoidable rite of passage for any self-respecting entertainer, no matter where they fit in the food chain. Sci-fi retro styling? Make mine a large one, and be quick with it. Bryan Ferry knew this thirty years ago, when he decided to suddenly launch himself as the most glamorous playboy in pop. Not only a radical architect of glam rock back in the early 1970s, Ferry for the past three decades also has been King

Cool, an effortless ambassador of the good life. When Ferry's Roxy Music first appeared, at the very start of the 1970s, they were so different from their peers that they may as well have been from outer space.

Was this the man who was going to help me escape suburbia?

Roxy's music was certainly arresting—pop art Americana mixed with searing R&B and avant-garde electronics—but it was their clothes that really turned heads. Leopard skin and snakeskin. Gold lamé. Pink leather. At a time when most pop groups thought long hair, cowboy boots, and denim were the height of sartorial elegance, Ferry and his band walked into the world looking like renegade spacemen. Boys loved them, and eventually girls did too. The right boys, and the right girls, of course. The first Roxy Music album—cunningly called *Roxy Music*—is like a whirlwind of playful decadence, a members-only nightclub with Ferry as the quintessential playboy making a bumblebee exit, buzzing from table to table on his way out.

Roxy were a montage of hot music, giddy drunken laughter, stoic posing, and nightclub reverie. The music took the old sweet rock 'n' roll melodies and twisted them like hairpins. It was symphony strictly of artifice, and all the better for it. If you happened to grow up in the 1970s in England, then you couldn't ignore Roxy. You could adore them or resist them, but never ignore them. When I was a teenager in the early 1970s, Roxy were my world. It wasn't a world I particularly understood, and certainly not one I could decipher, yet I knew I wanted it badly. It was a seemingly classless world full of bright lights and dark alleys, of loose women wearing tight dresses and very bad men wearing very good suits. This was a glamorous world etched with danger, a full-scale escape from reality, a world full of rich people pretending to be poor, and poor people pretending to be rich. And Roxy were its fulcrum, the very zenith of style centrale. I spent a lot of time with Bryan Ferry when I was young, and although his words described things I had never experienced, and thought I probably never would, I felt close to him, close enough to share gum.

My friend Alix went overboard in describing them, but I knew what he meant: " . . . crossing the greasy campness of 1950s Teddy Boy narcissism with the satin-tat and feather boas of the Charleston-era 1930s, mixed up with a dash of 1970s androgyny and 1920s sci-fi, and fired through some kind of Kensington High Street drag-queen particle accelerator, so that it positively glowed like fluorescent Biba lip gloss."

Yep, that's what I wanted alright.

It was another ten years before I met my hero. I was twenty-four and thought I was over compliments, whether from men, women, or pop stars. Especially pop stars. The year was 1985 and I had been commissioned to interview Ferry, to publicize his first solo LP since the 1970s. Even though I was fast approaching my mid-twenties, I still had a crushed-velvet soft spot for the man who had turned an affected, withdrawn twelve-year-old into an affected, withdrawn twelve-year-old with an unhealthy interest in snakeskin jackets and 1950s American kitsch. And at the time I might not have been able to copy his jet-black duck's-tail quiff, but I could pretend to sing in French as well as anyone in my class (*"Jamais, jamais, jamais!"*).

Rather annoyingly, it had been arranged that I would meet the aging crooner at his Chelsea offices early one Sunday morning. For some reason, which I have far too much hindsight to recall, I had spent the previous evening in a seedy Mayfair nightclub wearing a bright red velvet drape coat, a garish pink shirt with elaborate ruffles, and a pair of voluminous custom-built trousers made from dozens of different pieces of violently clashing tartan. At three o'clock in the morning I no doubt looked as presentable as anyone else in a seedy Mayfair nightclub, but at nine the following day, stumbling down the King's Road, having spent the night God knows where, I must have looked an absolute fright (come on, I know I did).

But dear old Bryan didn't think so, and if he did he didn't let on. Oh no. After a few polite exchanges he looked down at the material covering my legs and said, in an incredulous whisper I have never forgotten, "My God, those are the most amazing trousers I have ever seen."

Now, even though I know that this could have been just another example of Ferry's notorious charm, I was quite shocked at my reaction. The singer had disarmed me so much that the interview was a mere formality. (Even by this stage of my career, I had interviewed a lot of famous people, but Ferry was the only one who had caused the hairs on the back of my neck to spring up when he walked in the room.) There was no way I could ask him anything remotely challenging (Why had he bothered ruining "Jealous Guy"? Why had he emasculated Roxy?) as I was still beaming at the memory of these casually delivered words of praise.

Looking back on this, I suppose I shouldn't have been too surprised. Who wouldn't want to get a compliment from Bryan Ferry? He certainly wasn't expecting one in return. And anyway, who gives Bryan Ferry compliments?

Much like me, Ferry had longed for escape as a boy. Having grown up in the northeast of England in a fairly impoverished mining village called Washington, near Durham, Ferry was desperate to travel south, to London, where everyone goes, to metropolitan excess. He was helped in his cause by the legendary pop artist Richard Hamilton, who taught Ferry at Newcastle University. I got taught by a mad French woman in green fishnet tights, and Bryan Ferry gets Richard Hamilton! Hamilton not only inspired the Roxy Music "cover girl" album covers, but he also inspired the music itself, a mixture of sci-fi aspiration and 1950s Americana. "To go that route seemed the only option," said Ferry. "I mean, we could've had a picture of a band, looking rather glum, which was normal, standing on a cobbled street or something. But I didn't fancy that. The pinup was a great way to sell things traditionally, whether it was a Cadillac or a Coke bottle or a packet of cigarettes."

Or even Roxy Music, come to think of it.

In 1957, Hamilton came up with a definitive description of pop art, one that could easily apply to Roxy itself, and one that Ferry took to heart: "Popular (designed for a mass audience), transient (short-term solution), expendable (easily forgotten), low cost, mass-produced, young (aimed at youth), sexy, gimmicky, glamorous, big business." Throw in some 1950s balladry, white noise, and synthesizer treatments, plus some futuristic teddy boys, and there you have Ferry's vision. Even their name was pop: "We made a list of about twenty names for groups," said Ferry. "We thought it should be magical or mystical but not mean anything, like cinema names, Locarno, Gaumont, Rialto." According to Andy Mackay, Roxy's redoubtable sax player, "If Roxy Music had been like cooking, it would be like a dish in Marinetti's *Futurist Cookbook*, Car Crash: a hemisphere of puréed dates and a hemisphere of puréed anchovies, which are then stuck together in a ball and served in a pool of raspberry juice. I mean, it's virtually inedible, but it can be done." A fashion grenade rather than a fashion parade (Roxy were roughly analogous to a Gucci or a Chanel, only with a yard of fake leopard skin and a sachet of sequins thrown in for good measure), without them there would have been no Prince, no Culture Club, no Duran Duran, no Suede, no Pulp, no Blur, no Franz Ferdinand. And probably no me.

From the age of thirteen all I ever wanted to do was go to art school. These days I sometimes wish I'd actually paid attention at school, applied myself more to business studies, and ended up in the City. But I didn't. I was obsessed with David Hockney, Andy Warhol, David Bowie, *Interview* magazine, and all those travel books I found in the local library full of photographs of Main Street America. Billboards, Coca-Cola signs, Las Vegas swimming pools, palm trees, traffic lights, backlit Perspex shop signs, the cluttered skylines of Los Angeles and Detroit. Americana, that was what I was in love with, an Americana seen through the quizzical eyes of pop art and trashy pop, Tom Wolfe and Vance Packard.

And what I loved about the whole idea of Roxy Music was the fact that it wasn't the sound of bedroom doors being slammed, it wasn't the sound of youthful market-town angst or adolescent frustration . . . it was the sound of aspiration, travel, power . . . sex. It was a modern-day love letter to an anglicized America, a 1970s idea of 1950s space nobility. They—we!—were conquering the new frontier. In silver jumpsuits! Playing guitars! In front of girls!

To an adolescent boy in suburban Southeast England, Roxy's B-movie dreams were unbelievably glamorous, and as my father got posted from nondescript small town to nondescript small town—in Norfolk, Suffolk, Buckinghamshire, Lincolnshire, Cambridgeshire, Berkshire, Kent, from RAF quarter to half-timbered bungalow to pebbledash semi—my itinerant existence (which is what we all had before we had a lifestyle) was accompanied at all times by Bryan Ferry, David Bowie, and the extravagant fantasies of my future life. I painted, I drew, I meticulously designed cities, cars, and magazines with felt-tips and Sellotape. And I played records, all the time, from the moment I got up to the moment I went to sleep. I'd fall asleep listening to Roxy's "Virginia Plain" or Frank Sinatra's "Night and Day." I was one of those twelve-year-olds who saw Bowie perform "Starman" on *Top of the Pops*, one of those twelve-year-olds who, having seen this, would forever be in love with the idea of pop music, whose idea of glamour and sophistication was bound up in a flame-haired rock 'n' roller with thigh-high boots and wonky teeth.

Spurred on by Bowie and Ferry, I got my hair cut in an approximation of Ziggy Stardust's, bought half a dozen pairs of glitter socks (I can still remember them: red, yellow, black, pale blue, purple, and silver), and got into tank tops, butterfly-collared shirts, Oxford bags, and velvet jackets with aircraft-carrier lapels. Suddenly I was a space-age juvenile delinquent with knobs on.

Although we didn't know it at the time, we were the first postmodern generation, while Roxy Music—obviously, dumb-o!—were the first postmodern pop group. Before Roxy Music, fashion hated rock and rock hated fashion. Ferry courted the art-school crowd and paid lip service to the fashion industry while never forgetting the denim-clad punters who paid his wages. Clever move, but one that never endeared the band to America. Although America informed pretty much everything they did, Roxy never made it there, as the great swathes between New York and Los Angeles didn't get their homegrown art-school camp, didn't get their weird songs or their getup. What the hell was a "Pyjama-rama" anyway? For Roxy, success in America was like trying to catch a fly with chopsticks. Why would they understand Bryan Ferry when they were obsessed with the Eagles?

Essentially Ferry discovered his own identity via the assumption of false ones, in a bid, perhaps, to spend the rest of his life in a world full of Roxy Music album covers. Using a little bit of Billy Fury, a little bit of Biba, and a soupçon of good old-fashioned music hall, Ferry reinvented himself as a glittering, larger-than-need-be playboy. And boy did he love his job. He was brazen in his lust for a life that was never really meant to be his. He wanted not just the fast cars and the fast women, but also the kudos that came with them. It wasn't enough for him to be seen enjoying himself, people had to believe that he meant it, that these things for him were not merely confetti—they were food and drink.

Roxy, meanwhile, were the perfect vehicle, a hard-edged, driving rock band who understood the importance of flash. If Ferry was the fruit and flowers, Roxy themselves were the bricks and mortar, a bunch of talented musos who were prepared to let Ferry take them where he wanted to go. Of course there was also Brian Eno, the frenzied genius who famously left the band after their second album, *For Your Pleasure*; and while many critics say the fire went out of Roxy's engine when Eno moved on, their third album, *Stranded*, from 1973, is their one true masterpiece, containing Ferry's very best three songs, the three my iPod is never, ever without: "Serenade," "A Song for Europe," and "Mother of Pearl" (a song that perfectly encapsulates his ambivalent feelings toward the world he had invented for himself).

Having dissolved Roxy in 1975, and then again in the early 1980s, Ferry has been solo for twenty years. He has made albums that are so polished they practically rubbed him away, albums of cover versions, movie soundtracks, and has had the occasional hit. He still plays gigs at stately homes, sometimes with Roxy, sometimes alone. He now wears little but Savile Row, flits around the fringes of London society, and enjoys the company of young girls. Still something of a role model, he is a fiftysomething roué, and at an age when many men are considering just exactly where to lay their laurels, and wondering where they left their slippers, the elder statesman of glam rock still dusts off his Antony Price tuxedo, musses up his considerable raven-black thatch, and takes himself to town.

I last saw him a year or so ago, in the front row at a Gucci fashion show in Milan. He was sitting, quietly, crouched in a heavy cashmere overcoat, as though he wasn't especially bothered about attracting the attention of the photographers. The front row has huge redemptive powers and can grab a celebrity back from the clutches of obscurity in the time it takes to snap a picture with a mobile phone. It's also the yardstick by which a designer's show is measured, although Ferry didn't seem interested in either fact. He is, after all, now a fully paid-up English gent, with manners to match. As I took my place next to him and turned to introduce myself, he gently touched my knee and said, "I know, Dylan. We've met. In 1985. You were wearing the most amazing pair of trousers. You didn't think I'd forget, did you?"

5

Build It and They Will Come

How Jonathan Ive and Steve Jobs made the iPod

It's only a small, three-panel cartoon, yet it speaks volumes about its subject. Panel one is captioned "The road to Cupertino" and features two spiky-haired religious devotees, dressed appropriately in Buddhist-monk-like garb, trudging through the forest. "We're almost there, mate!" says the first. "Almost *where*, Ivan?! You said we were going to a conference."

In the second panel our two compadres are sitting in a crowd of similarly dressed geeks listening to an address from a fellow disciple. "We're going to do way more than that!" says our first friend. "We've come to pay homage to 'The One' . . . and I would appreciate if you referred to me as iVan with a small *i* from now on." "The One?" replies his friend.

Panel three is captioned "The One they call Ive" and features a picture of designer Jonathan Ive, sitting in the lotus position, arms folded, dressed only in a robe, levitating over one of his creations.

For many of his generation, and for most of the one behind him, Ive is nothing less than a deity. Ostensibly he spends most of his time sticking bits of metal and plastic together, but he is treated as something of a demigod. Ive is the most revered designer of the modern age, a sort of Warhol for the digital generation, if Warhol had been a shorn-haired muscle-bound industrial designer from Essex, that is. As vice president of industrial design at Apple, Ive has combined what he describes as "fanatical care beyond the obvious stuff" and relentless experiments into new tools, materials, and production processes, to design such groundbreaking products as the iMac, the iBook, and the PowerBook G4. It is perhaps fitting for the man the *New York Times* described as "perhaps the most influential designer in the computer world" to have achieved media ubiquity before the age of forty, but what is slightly more unusual is the list of nicknames he's earned. He has more than your average pop star: the Armani of Apple, the Beckham of design, Mr. Mac, Apple Man . . . Even Bono—a fan for years before Ive created a special black U2 iPod for the launch of *How to Dismantle an Atomic Bomb*—came up with one for him: Johnny iPod.

"Jonathan's designs have touched millions of people's lives and transformed the workplace," says fashion designer Paul Smith, echoing what many in the entertainment, technology, and fashion industries think of him. His products are not just the same old things packaged to look new; they actually are new. They are objects no one would have imagined ten years ago, which reach beyond the technical and aesthetic constraints of the twentieth century. Which is why Jonathan Ive is the first great designer of the twenty-first century.

Born in Chingford in Essex in 1967 ("please tell people it's not Chigwell . . . they always say it's Chigwell," he says with a smile), Ive is the son of a silversmith who became a teacher and then Ofsted inspector for design and technology. It wasn't just indoctrination that caused Ive to be interested in design, though; from an early age he was pulling things apart to see how they fit back together again—toys, radios, cassette players, anything to do with music.

"By the age of thirteen or fourteen I was pretty certain that I wanted to draw and make stuff," he says. "I knew that I wanted to design but I had no idea what I'd design as I was interested in everything: cars, furniture, jewelery, boats, products of all kinds. After visiting a few design consultancies I eventually decided that product design would be a pretty good foundation as it seemed the most general."

When he left school, he decided he wanted to design cars and enrolled in a course at Central St. Martins in London but found it too challenging. The other students were "too weird. They were making 'vroom vroom' noises as they did their drawings." And so he ended up at Newcastle Polytechnic, studying product design. Newcastle was slower than London, less frenetic, less transient (with no one making "vroom vroom" noises); it was a place he could think, a place he could forge a career.

Which he did. Toward the end of the eighties he came south to cofound the London-based industrial design consultancy Tangerine, where he helped develop everything from TVs and VCRs to sanitaryware and hair combs. Ive likes to tell the story of how, one gray day, he drove up to Hull to present a new toilet to Ideal Standard. It happened to be Comic Relief Day and the firm's head of marketing sat through the entire presentation wearing a big red plastic nose. Ive's designs were rejected.

At Tangerine he also worked on the development of the 1991 PowerBook for Apple (which had hired Ive's company as external consultants), the earliest version of the machine this book is written on. While working on the PowerBook, he became frustrated at the arbitrary nature of the intended design; he thought the industry was suffering from "creative bankruptcy" and that Apple should take the lead by spending more time developing the external forms of its products. Apple listened, and a year later he was working there as director of design. Initially reluctant to embrace the company, he slowly started to fall in love with Apple, which at least appeared to know what good design was, even if it wasn't always so good at using it.

"I started to learn more about the company, how it had been founded, its values and its structure," says Ive. "The more I learned about this cheeky, almost rebellious company, the more it appealed to me, as it unapologetically pointed to an alternative in a complacent industry.

"I hated computers when I was at Poly, but I assumed it was my problem, that I was somehow inept. But in my last year there I discovered Macs and they spoke to me. They said so much about the company, and about the product itself. Essentially it wasn't a crappy computer, which is what I had been used to up until then."

When he says "Apple really was born to innovate," you get the feeling he's really talking about himself.

However, it wasn't until Steve Jobs returned to the company that Ive was given the freedom to concentrate on the "pursuit of nothing other than good design." Then steering a company—his company—that had been diluted by a "design by focus group" mentality, Jobs realized that he needed people like Ive to reinvent Apple. And so began the iMac project.

The translucent turquoise iMac was launched in 1998, and on the first weekend of its release, Apple sold over 150,000 of them. With its unified curvaceous organic form, it looked as though it had been shipped in from a nearby film lot, maybe from the set of a digital-retro remake of *2001: A Space Odyssey*. Not only did it break all conventions in terms of what a computer should actually look like, but it also had a character all its own, one that shouted cool. It wasn't a PC, it wasn't made by Microsoft . . . and yes, it *was* cool. Spurred on by a high-profile ad campaign—"Chic, not Geek"—the iMac became the best-selling computer in America. When Steve Jobs launched the first Apple computer, it was not supplied with a case, so hobbyists had to construct their own, many from wood. The iMac was nothing *but* case.[3]

Not only did it help shore up Apple by selling more than two million units in its first year, the iMac transformed product design by introducing color and light to the drab "greige" world of computing, where, until its arrival, new products were routinely encased in opaque gray or beige plastic.

"There's no other product that changes function like the computer," says Ive. "The iMac can be a jukebox, a tool for editing video, a way to organize photographs. You can design on it, write on it. Because what it does is so new, so

---

[3]There is a popular urban design myth indulged by the camouflage-trouser-wearing boffins of Silicone Valley that plagues both Jobs and Ive. The gist is that Apple had actually designed the iMac years earlier but that the existing design chiefs were not interested, so it was put away, in one of the many ante rooms that snake around Apple's giant glass atrium in Cupertino. When Jobs returned from the wilderness and asked what ideas they had been working on—what stillborn computers, what design tabulations— Ive is alleged to have pulled it out of the iBin, and the rest is iHistory.

changeable, it allows us to use new materials, to create new forms. The possibilities are endless. I love that."

Computers used to sit behind plateglass windows in specially refrigerated purpose-built offices and were tended to by bespectacled boffins in white overcoats. They were cumbersome and expensive and were used principally to crunch numbers. But when IBM ignored the demand for "minicomputers"—i.e., what we basically think of now as a computer—it opened the floodgates to a generation of young, long-haired entrepreneurs. Like Steve Jobs. Jobs wasn't interested in producing mainframes, as these big computers were called; he wanted to concentrate on minis, exploiting transistor technology by making smaller and smaller machines—machines that looked like they belonged in the home, machines that looked happy to be at home.

Jonathan Ive wanted similar things.

The first modern computers arrived in the late 1940s, with IBM quickly establishing itself as the main player on the commercial side. It was so successful, so omnipotent, and so far ahead of its rivals that in the early 1950s the industry was popularly defined as "IBM and the seven dwarfs." It was a hegemony that survived until Microsoft began to spread its tentacles. And it was Microsoft that Apple needed to attack. If Apple couldn't do it by critical mass—in the eighties Microsoft began to dominate the PC market in a way no company had ever done before—then the company would have to do it with design. Which, to a certain extent, it had always done. In the seventies, Apple started telling anyone who would listen that it was at the intersection of technology and the arts—that's how the company described itself, as having one foot in the sixties and one in the eighties. Its manifestos were sprinkled around like confetti on the

Thanksgiving parade: (1) Ease and simplicity, simplicity and ease; (2) caring beyond the functional imperative; (3) acknowledging that products have a significance way beyond the traditional views of function.

But Ive is not just a decorator, which is why he has always had such a problem with those who simply imitate the form of his designs. Ive is an industrial designer, and the inner workings of his machines are as fundamental to his peace of mind as the arched back of the iBook or the translucent glow of his jelly iMacs. How could he make things quicker, simpler, smaller? He thought back to how things used to be, back in the days when the success of a computer was determined by how small it was (much like calculators and mobile phones). If an integrated circuit of transistors looked like the wiring diagram of an office building inscribed on the nail of your little toe, then surely circuits could soon be found inside everything from rocket ships to stereos. Surely it would soon be possible to make one—well, maybe more than one, maybe a million—small enough to fit on the head of a pin!

Ive's brain works in similar, steadfast ways, making the art of the impossible the only game in town.

This Essex-boy-made-good doesn't look much like a talismanic figure. His seventy-hour work weeks mean his pallor is largely untouched by the Californian sun, and in his tight, gun-metal gray T-shirt, indigo jeans, hybrid running shoes, and swarthy head stubble, Ive looks less like a techie nerd and more like a Midwestern jock. His only concession to the designer fetishism he has helped foster since he has been at Apple is his watch: a smart piece of precision engineering on a white natural-rubber strap designed by his friend, the similarly enigmatic Marc Newson. Walking down the street in his adopted home of San Francisco, Ive could easily be mistaken for one of the city's omnipresent bike messengers (either that, or a tourist from Hoxton). But his casual appearance belies his hallowed position at the very heart of corporate America, or at least what passes for corporate America in the twenty-first century. One should never forget that while Ive is a hero to the combat-pants-wearing Internet generation, he is a new media executive who pulls in more than two million a year.

A reluctant speaker, Ive comes across as deadpan and rather droll. He is self-deprecating to the point of absurdity, and the only time you'll hear him use the word "I" is when he's talking about one of the products he helped make famous. Ask him a simple question and he can launch into a monologue, giving you a passionate twenty-minute tour of a new computer's design, or how the lid closes on a particular model of the PowerBook, or how the intensity of the backlight affects your mood.

Ive lives in a pretty but small two-bedroom house in the Twin Peaks district of San Francisco with his wife, Heather—a writer and aspiring novelist he met while at college in Newcastle—and their young children. He devours the British TV comedies his friends send him (when it was first broadcast, he became an obsessive fan of *The Office*), although most of his downtime is spent either listening to or making music. Affectations seem to bore him, and while he loves the sushi here, he misses the curries in London's Brick Lane. Free time is spent "living a serene life." This consists of dabbling with techno-pop, computer-generated music, and relaxing with colleagues (though he's a collaborator at work, his music allows him to fastidiously work on things alone). And after a string of sensible Saabs and vintage

Jaguars, Ive's current toy is a £150,000 Aston Martin DB7, his only really ostentatious possession. He uses it principally for the weekday fifty-mile commute to the Apple HQ in Cupertino, although he says he bought it largely because of his long-standing interest in car design rather than any attempt to be a show-off.

He is obsessed by details, or at least the prospect of eliminating them. To wit: No screws around the edge of any Apple computer screen, no hook interfering with the view of the display on Apple laptops, and as few knobs, buttons, and lights as possible. Ive and his team take great pride in simplifying their products, getting rid of extraneous clutter, and solving prosaic problems so the consumer doesn't have to. Attention to minutiae is his métier: the suspended Sleep state on a Mac was once indicated by a slowly flashing light, but Ive soon changed that. The light now pulses slowly, as though the machine were actually breathing.

Clive Grinyer, a former colleague at Tangerine who now works for telecom giant Orange, first met Ive in 1988. "We hit it off immediately, and he invited me to Newcastle. He built a hundred models for his final project at Poly, a system of hearing aids for teachers and deaf pupils in schools. Normally students would make five or six models at most. He had refined it so much that you realized he was totally dedicated to his art."

When he made a pen for a Japanese company, he built in what he called a "fiddle factor" because he knew that was what people liked to do with their pens. One anecdote rivals *Spinal Tap* in its madness: at Tangerine he once spent an afternoon choosing between fifteen shades of black for a computer. He even consulted candy manufacturers in an attempt to discover how to make the plastic casing for the iMac both blue and transparent.

Ive pours invention and elegance into his products: The first iMac was a gumdrop-inspired solution to making an all-in-one machine. The second, with its movable flat screen, alluded to a sunflower. The popular transparent Apple mouse came from his thinking about how drops of water sit on a flat surface. An angle-poise desk lamp helped inspire one version of the iMac. The see-through outer casing of the iBook came from how food looks when wrapped in cling film.

And none of them are gimmicks. "I don't want to design things that the world doesn't need," he says. Because he has been so plagiarized, he has a heightened sense of purpose and dislikes designers who use "swoopy shapes to look good, stuff that is so aggressively designed, just to catch the eye. I think that's arrogance; it's not done for the benefit of the user."

To almost everything he touches, Jonathan Ive attaches his prefix, the *i*. It infers modernity, cool, edge, and has now been appropriated by a generation of carpetbaggers who use it in much the same they used *.com* in the late nineties. Ive's transparent plastic iMac, the iBook, the G4 Cube, and the Titanium PowerBook are cultural icons. They single-handedly remind us of the power of sophisticated, sexy design. With the original iMac, launched in 1998, he created the first object of desire and affection, in effect feminizing what had hitherto been a masculine product. Suddenly computers were no longer defined in terms of process and speed, but also in terms of color, form, and tactility. If you own any household items in jelly-colored plastic, for instance, or have bought into the fad of household goods made of heavy, transparent plastic, you own something influenced by him. But staying one step ahead of the competition isn't just a part of his design brief; it's part of the Apple DNA. The breathing Sleep button is not the sort of thing Microsoft makes.

But it is Jonathan Ive through and through. Toward the end of the nineties, he started to get serious acclaim, began to be heralded as this "signifier," this beacon of applied creativity, a veritable guru of the age. He was voted the best this, the most influential that, the man most likely to do . . . whatever it was we expected of him. As soon as we consumers started to realize that design was sexy and, with the application of technology, was about to project us into this brave new world, one decorated in all the trendy ergonomic nonsense we could possibly want, we all started wondering who was going to show us around. It didn't seem right to embrace the social commentators and media consultants we had trusted for the past couple of decades—surely we should put our faith in the sort of people who actually got their hands dirty, who actually knew how all this worked, who actually had a hand in making this stuff. People—someone—like Jonathan Ive.

He wasn't just a postmodern geek either—he'd been awarded the highest British design honor with his appointment to the RSA's Faculty of Royal Designers for Industry—how could you beat that? There were only two hundred members, and Ive was right up there with architect Norman Foster, furniture designer Ron Arad, and fashion designers Paul Smith and John Galliano. Not bad, eh? He was a rock 'n' roll tech-head, if that wasn't a contradiction in terms. How cool!

Up until the beginning of 2001, Ive had fundamentally

been playing around—successfully—with form. He hadn't been reinventing the wheel; he'd simply been making it smaller, trendier, and in a bunch of weird colors. Ive's wheel may have looked like a wheel from another planet, but it was still just a wheel. He had yet to turn his hand to something that actually invented, or defined, a product genre. An impossibly brilliant man, he himself didn't even know what was around the corner—not even he knew that the devotion he inspired in his disciples was going to get even more intense.

Not even Jonathan Ive knew he was going to have a hand in designing the first and maybe most important music carrier of the twenty-first century—and, in the process, changing the music industry forever.

In February 2001, a freelance engineer named Tony Fadell was skiing in Vail. As he carefully prepared to attack another black-diamond, run, his mobile rang. On the other end was Apple's hardware czar, Jon Rubinstein, who wasn't calling about Fadell's welfare. Rubinstein had just been charged by Steve Jobs to create a groundbreaking music player and to get it to market by Christmas that year. A groundbreaking music player . . . in ten months. Rubinstein had a list in front of him and Fadell listened intently. There were certain requirements: it had to look original, it had to have acute functionality (i.e., it had to work a hell of a lot better than all the other digital music players out there, the ones that weren't really working at all, according to the feedback the technicians were getting), it had to have an extremely fast connection to computers (via Apple's superfine high-speed FireWire standard) so songs could be quickly uploaded, it had to have downloading capability, it had to dovetail with the company's recently introduced iTunes software, and, most important, it had to look, feel, and act exactly like every other successful Apple product. It had to be hot and cool at the same time. Very hot and very, very cool.

It was, in short, a challenge, but then Fadell was on top of a mountain, and things looked pretty good. "Why can't I build a digital music player?" he thought to himself as he stared across the sky, feeling quietly invincible. Everyone else was launching digital music players, so why wasn't Apple? It was easy now, now that the industry was coming to grips with MP3s. We've known about them for ages—let's use 'em.

MP3s were invented by a group of German scientists in 1987 as a way of shrinking video files so they could be run on computers. By stripping away as much data as possible—all the stuff that theoretically listeners and viewers don't notice—they created manageable files that contained less information but were perfectly acceptable to the human eye and ear, files that were usually one twelfth the size of the original file (roughly, one minute of audio data equals 1 MB of space at 128 Kps—kilobits, the measurement of audio data storage space used by a piece of music per second of its downloading). As the technology actually compressed files, they obviously were not CD quality, and in some cases they were not even cassette quality, even though everyone said they were; the loss of quality was discernable when the files were amplified, but on headphones? No problem. On headphones MP3s were just fine, more than just fine actually—they were just fucking fantastic! People would say, "Have you heard this stuff! Here, take a listen!"

And after the code was approved by the International Standards Organization, these files became known as ISO-

MPEG Audio Layer-3s, or MP3s for short. And there they stayed, waiting to be exploited by Steve Jobs.

Fadell didn't make his decision there and then, but by the time he was at the foot of the mountain, even though he was feeling slightly less invincible, he could see the possibilities. He had been given carte blanche to draw on all of Apple's senior staff, including Jobs himself, so what was there to lose? That day Fadell skipped his après-ski, called Rubinstein back, and started thinking. Two months later, ensconced in his glass bunker in Infinite Loop, the Apple HQ in Cupertino, he was well on his way. Crucially, Apple senior vice president Phil Schiller came up with the idea of a scroll wheel that accelerated as your finger spun it, making it easier for you to work your way through the menus and playlists and song titles. As for its memory, a few hard drive players already existed, but most were large and bulky. To develop the iPod, Apple initially bought the entire inventory of a new generation of smaller drives from Toshiba, making the iPod the smallest and sleekest hard drive player in the market. Apple was quick to reject flash memory chips, the most common technology used in music players, as they were only able to hold a few dozen songs. They may have been cheap but weren't of interest to Jobs—he wanted a machine that could hold *thousands* of tunes.

Then Jonathan Ive, Apple's industrial designer, came up with the case, a groundbreaking piece of kit that was smaller than anything else on the market. "From early on we wanted a product that would seem so natural and so inevitable and so simple you almost wouldn't think of it as having been designed," says Ive. And he insisted it be white, Apple white: "It's neutral, but it is a bold neutral, just shockingly neutral."

The design, or rather, the shape, was incidental—it just

happened that way. "It could have been shaped like a banana if we'd wanted," says Ive.

Instead it looked like a cigarette pack for those addicted to music instead of tobacco. A cigarette pack in cocaine white.

It was made, crucially, from twin-shot plastic. From a processing point of view it became possible to do things with plastic that had never been done before. Twin-shooting materials—molding different plastics together or comolding plastic to metal—gave the engineers a range of functional and formal opportunities that didn't really exist before. The machine had no fasteners and no battery doors, making it possible to create something that was completely sealed.

According to Ive, the product had a natural birth, and although he'd never use the vernacular, it was a no-brainer:

"We are unique that we have an OS [operating system] as well as hardware," he says. "On top of this, the components were coming into alignment. We had jukebox software, and hard drives were getting smaller, so it was design and technology coming together in a perfect way. We made the iPod as simple as we possibly could, especially on the inside. It really annoys me when people say that simplicity is a style, because it's not; it's not a veneer. Simplification is one of the most difficult things to do. Also, for the iPod to be successful, it has to be part of a large complicated system—it has to be hooked up to a computer of some sort, plus it needs all the software. The iPod just navigates and retrieves data.

"In a way, the interface became the icon of the product."

Naturally, most of the initial drawings and designs for the iPod were produced on a Mac. How could it be any other way?

Jobs was being evangelical about this product, a product that was still in the very earliest stages of design. He was running around telling everyone how good it was going to be, even though he knew little about it. When quizzed beyond his knowledge, he would give a withering look and quote Darwin: "It is not the strongest of the species that survive, nor the most intelligent, but the one most responsive to change." Jobs wanted a machine that defined the market, a machine that was able to handle all the music you wanted to hear (just how much could you really squeeze onto a portable?), something that was simple to use (the competition's machines were ugly and confusing), and something that was quintessentially Apple. Which is what he got. Jobs has a tendency to send his pet projects back to the drawing board as they're nearing completion, a sign, perhaps, of his perfectionism or his inability to let go. "It's happened on every Pixar movie," Jobs confesses. But when he finally saw the prototype, several months later, he said, "It's as Apple as anything Apple has ever done."

And Apple didn't create just a portable jukebox for all your music (Jesus, have you seen this? It can Hoover up all your CDs. It's like listening to your own greatest hits! I just fed my entire music collection into this thing and I can't believe it ate the whole thing! It's like *Little Shop Of Horrors!* You just gotta get one!). The iPod does loads of other neat stuff too: it can be used as a clock, as a diary for synchronizing appointments, for digital voice recording ("Hello Cleveland!"), for downloading data, and for photo storage. The iPod is a true breakthrough product. Other MP3-playback devices take forever to load music since they use relatively slow USB (Universal Serial Bus) for data transfer, have limited capacity since they use solid-state memory, and are clunky and ungainly since they weren't crafted by Ive's Industrial Design Group (Ive may like to say otherwise, but his job has always been to curve edges and miniaturize). They are ugly, ugly, ugly! The 6.5-ounce iPod's huge 5 GB hard drive could be filled with approximately a thousand near-CD quality songs in ten minutes through its fast FireWire port, and seamless integration with iTunes 2.0 made synchronizing music libraries a snap. Backed by a ten-hour battery life, the iPod is essentially an all-day record shop you can fold neatly into your pocket. It has an equalizer to adjust the volume of anything you download, and you can read the instructions in Spanish, French, or Italian. It has twenty minutes of skip protection. Hell, you can even listen to it on your stereo—all you have to do is buy a headphone plug to composite audio cable (the white-and-yellow-and-red-pronged cord you use to connect your TV and DVD together) and just sit back and wallow. How fucking cool is that! It is just so damned neat. Even the scroll wheel guy Philip Schiller said so: "iPod is going to change the way people listen to music."

As for its name, this new beast had been christened before it was born: the *i* for *Internet*, plus the acronym for *portable open database*—the *i* and the *Pod* were fused, in keeping with the fashion for jamming names together, with an uppercase letter sticking up in the middle ("as if creating some hyperhard alloy for the twenty-first century," said Tom Wolfe).

And then they launched it. On November 10, two months after 9/11. Not only was it birthed into a country already deep in mourning, but also the bottom had fallen out of the tech market (hell, for months the bottom fell out of all markets). The iPod was criticized for being expensive—$399—and for the fact that it was only compatible with Macintosh, a computer owned by fewer than a twentieth of consumers.

And it didn't hold that many songs (wasn't a thousand enough, guys?) or have a compatible online music store to download from. Apart from that it was perfect.

"We applied a design philosophy to a product we didn't have, to a product we wanted desperately," says Jonathan Ive. "You have to remember—and this is very important— that there's a lot of us at Apple that like music, who actually like music a lot. It's as simple as that. Although we had a brief to make a music player, at Apple things are not always as premeditated as they appear. Another thing you have to remember is that our goal is not to make money, our goal is to make the very best consumer products so that we can then make a lot of money. That might sound naïve, but that's why I go to work every day."

The advertising of the product was crucial, and needed to set the machine apart from everything else in the market. Apple's brief to New York–based ad agency TBWA/Chiat/Day was simple: empower the individual. Unlike every other aspect of the computer world, the iPod had little to do with togetherness, had little to do with community spirit. The iPod was all about individuality and personal space, and its marketing would soon reflect that. Chiat Day's most successful ads for the machine revolved around "iPod-World"—a place that you, and only you, could visit—and had bright, pop-colored backgrounds, and in the foreground individuals seen only in silhouette (so as not to alienate the consumer—you, them, us!). And curling through the posters were those little telltale white headphones, the tiny signifiers of a secret society, that only we, and we alone, knew about. Where were we? We were in our own little worlds, listening to our own private soundtracks in our own particular way. To reinforce the idea that Apple was selling an idea rather than a product, the ads appeared on flyers, bus stops, and billboards, as though they were advertising a new movie or a band. Clever, that.

Design aficionados and Apple geeks loved the iPod, and as soon as Apple got its act together and began upgrading it—which it did almost immediately—interest began to grow and grow. Apple then produced a version that was able to run on Windows, successfully launched an online version of iTunes, and in less than a year had secured a whopping 70 percent market share. Jobs had done it. This wasn't just another ruby in the crown—this was the crown itself. Quarterly sales soon reached 250,000 units, and then just eighteen months later ballooned to over 800,000, making the iPod the most successful digital music player in the world. In under three years! Soon people were calling it the Walkman of the twenty-first century, the Walkman of the digital generation, the Walkman that Sony forgot, and critical mass began to spread. According to U2 manager Paul McGuinness, "The iPod is to music what penicillin was to medicine."

Ask Jobs, and he will tell you we're about to enter the third phase of personal computing. The first era was all about utility—people using their thinking machines to do word processing, run spreadsheets, create desktop graphics, and the like. The second phase was about wiring all those machines together on the Internet and getting them to talk to each other. The third phase involves those same people using computers to orchestrate all the new digital gear that has steadily crept into their lives.

"We are surrounded by camcorders, digital cameras, MP3 players, Palms, cell phones, DVD players," says Jobs. "Some of these things are plenty useful without a personal computer. But a personal computer definitely enhances their

value. And several are completely unusable without a PC—
'a PC' meaning a Mac, in our case. We believe the next great
era is for the personal computer to be the hub of all these
devices."

This is all about "owning the whole widget," and it is the
vertical integration between iTunes (the software) and the
iPod (the hardware) that has been the key to Apple's success.
Because it owns "the widget" (all of it), Apple can control
the user experience from beginning to end.

"There are lots of examples where not the best product
wins," says Jobs. "Windows would be one of those, but there
are examples where the best product wins. And the iPod is a
great example of that."

iBondage, Up Yours! It's Time for Punk!

The Sex Pistols make a man of me

It's 1977, I'm seventeen, and I'm not allowed to like Isaac Hayes. I'm on the top floor of a huge squat in Camberwell, just about the least salubrious postcode in all of South London, and there's a party going on downstairs. It's four A.M. on a Sunday morning, and there are still about a hundred people in the basement, dancing away to the first two Ramones albums as though their lives depended on it.

Up here there are about a dozen punks, all lying on the floor, all smoking this amazingly strong grass and nodding sullenly at the ceiling. There's a small record player in the corner, which has just finished playing Patti Smith's *Horses*. And as no one appears to be the least bit bothered about replacing it, I root around in the stack of LPs lying against the wall, dig out Isaac Hayes's *Live at the Sahara Tahoe* and put it on.

It lasts for approximately eight seconds before a medium-sized, oxblood Doc Marten boot kicks it off.

"Take that shit off and put on the Stranglers!" says a

short, sharp girl with bloodshot eyes and peroxide feathered hair. "Disco sucks. Soul music is for fucking robots!"

Punk was as much of an apocalyptic catalyst for me as it was for many of my generation, and it shook me around, threw me up in the air, and—when I bounced back down again—forced me to confront my preconceptions about life, the universe, and everything in it. Well, at least the records I bought and the clothes I wore.

I have been in love with punk for exactly eighteen months, when I first heard the Ramones' "Beat on the Brat" at a house party in High Wycombe (one of those home counties towns that wishes it were a little bit closer to London). The next day I decided to turn myself into Johnny Ramone, and for the past year and a half have been walking around with a floppy, pudding-bowl haircut, drainpipe jeans, sneakers, a sailor top, and a (plastic) leather jacket. Overnight I turned from a neurotic boy outsider in an oversized overcoat and a hooded brow (clutching my Bob Dylan, Robert Wyatt, and Dean Martin albums under my arm) into the personification of a Bowery punk. Tell me this: how could you not fall in love with a group who displayed such a blatant disregard for sophistication as the Ramones? Whose bare-boned playing was matched only by their idiotic singing—the lyrics to "I Don't Wanna Walk Around with You" are four lines long, three of which are the same. When Joe Strummer, the lead singer of the Clash, approached the Ramones after seeing them play live in London in 1976, he was worried that his band's musicianship was still too rough for them to start recording. "Are you kidding?" Johnny said. "We're lousy, we can't play. If you wait until you can play, you'll be too old to get up there. We stink, really. But it's great."

But I am already living as though iTunes had already been invented. I believe that Frank Sinatra is just as important as the Sex Pistols, although no one agrees with me. In 1977 you either like the Clash and the Sex Pistols or you're the enemy. But can't you like everything? I do.

It's September and I've been in London for exactly six weeks, having left High Wycombe for Chelsea School of Art and the Ralph West Halls of Residence just south of the Kings Road, opposite Battersea Park. It is home to two hundred students, all of them studying some sort of arts degree at one of the big London art schools, and most of them in London for the first time. My room in Ralph West is another sanctuary, a place I can pretend is anywhere in the world. I am seventeen, and music is the most important thing in my life: more important than work, sex, family, everything. The Clash's next single (we've read in the *NME* it's "Clash City Rockers"!) is what's keeping me going. I know I've got some sort of practical exam next week, but to be honest I'm more interested in the Throbbing Gristle gig I'm going to on Sunday (in the end it was scary: they used dry ice and I thought they were gassing us). Last night we went to the Roxy for the first time, and although it wasn't very memorable (there was a no-mark punk band onstage who made the Dickies look like Sham 69), it was about as exciting as a gig can be. My life is defined by punk rock: I'm meant to be stretching some canvasses tomorrow morning, but I'm actually cadging a lift and going to buy some tickets for the festival at the 100 Club (the Jam, Adam and the Ants, etc.).

My sanctuary is all-denominational, and having spent an evening with Iggy Pop, the Ramones, or the Talking Heads (I remember one night in Linda Shearsby's room we played their '77 album six times in a row), I'd slink back to my room and play Joni Mitchell, Steely Dan, or Van Morrison. I didn't feel embarrassed, didn't feel as though I were letting the side down; for me it was perfectly natural. My room may have been covered with Sex Pistols posters, but my heart was elsewhere, in California, the deserts of Arizona, the West Coast of Ireland . . . Notting Hill in the late 1950s. On the perimeter of sleep I would lie there and imagine myself living the lives in those songs, believing my own life to be full of the same possibilities.

What no one ever remembers—or admits—about punk was the fact that we all liked other stuff too. And while it may have been convenient and cute and cool to pretend otherwise—"Hi, my name's Dylan and I am from the planet Year Zero and the first record I ever bought was 'Anarchy in the UK' "—none of us arrived in London fully formed. We all had baggage, all had a cupboard full of rattling, decaying skeletons. And my skeletons were holding about two dozen Frank Sinatra albums. Punk may have been the manifestation of disenfranchised youthful defiance, lathering up our seditious tendencies, but it was also a simple expression of adolescence: we liked it because we were young. Walking down the Kings Road on my way to Chelsea every morning, my head wasn't full of anarchy—it was full of hope. I wanted music to remind me of prosperity, not oppression, which is probably why I've never liked the blues.

The thing I remember most about punk was the violence, the fights: being barricaded by skinheads in the back of a church hall in Beaconsfield after a concert by a band called Deathwish; pint glasses being thrown at the Nashville;

fistfights in the doorway of the Marquee (the Jam again—
weren't we always going to see the Jam?).

And there is one evening I remember more than most. I
was in the upstairs toilets of the Rainbow, Finsbury Park,
some time in late 1977, as the Ramones thundered furiously
through their blitzkrieg bop downstairs. And up there, in the
relatively tranquil surroundings of the bathroom, Sid Vicious was exchanging punches and the occasional kick with
one of the Slits (Viv, Ari, Tessa? Who knew? Not me) whilst
I, with a relative nonchalance that was becoming dramatically less nonchalant with every well-aimed punch, was trying to get rid of four pints of hastily consumed, lukewarm,
overpriced lager.

They had tumbled in just as I was unzipping myself and,
after a few choice exchanges in vintage Anglo-Saxon (which
is what the pop fraternity used before discovering esturial
English), had set about each other with a ferocity reserved
only for the very passionate or the very drunk. I couldn't tell
which, and had no intention of finding out.

Oh my God, I thought, there he is, in all his feisty glory—
the trademark toilet-brush hairdo, the sneer, the lovingly
distressed biker's jacket, the drainpipe jeans, the intricately
torn Vivienne Westwood T-shirt, the bloody big boots . . .
and sooner or later, I thought, he is going to notice me.

When you're young the famous seem different. As you get
older, you quickly realize that they're unnervingly like normal people, with all the same banal fears and anxieties (only
with rather more engorged egos and expectations), but in
one's youth, the famous have the capacity to become unwieldy icons. Vicious was one such star. Punks might have
publicly eschewed the trappings of celebrity, but they were
still stars to us (they were still stars to themselves, if truth be

known), particularly if they happened to be a Sex Pistol. *Especially* if they were a Sex Pistol.

I'd had brushes with fame before: Adam Ant once spilled my pint as he pushed past me on his way to join the Ants on-stage at the 100 Club; a year earlier I'd help roadie for Generation X at the Nag's Head in High Wycombe; and the man who played drums on Johnny Wakelin's "In Zaire" (no, I don't remember it either) apparently lived three streets away from my mother.

But this was different. This was Sid Vicious, a genuine angry—and none-too-bright—young man. Of course I'd heard that he was a bit of a jerk (now and then he had the misfortune to come across as the Fonz's stupider cousin, usually when he opened his mouth), but he was still the bass player—and I use the term advisedly—with the most notorious bunch of ne'er-do-wells in the Western world. And he was standing four feet away from me.

The fight continued apace. It never occurred to me to try to interfere; in my eyes this would have been tantamount to suicide, and this particular Slit looked like she could punch and kick her way out of any altercation, even with a Sex Pistol—she certainly looked like she could knock the living daylights out of me.

Suddenly it was all over, and Sid's eyes turned in my direction. Oh my God! Surely he would suss me now, I thought (I was doing a lot of thinking that night). Surely he would see that I was nothing but a poseur, an art-school plastic punk who'd only recently thrown away his Tonto's Expanding Head Band albums (which I would have to buy again—at great expense—years later), and his flares (which I wouldn't).

My fear was palpable. Would he see me for what I was,

pick me up by the lapels of my black leather (okay, okay, *plastic*) jacket, spit in my eye, and throw me against the wall, snorting in disgust whilst condemning me for once owning a Jackson Browne LP? Would I have an extraordinary tale to tell the next day at college, or become a news item in the tabloids? ("Foul-mouthed punk rocker Sid razors Chelsea art student in nightclub toilet!")? No. I wasn't famous, you see, just another paranoid spotty seventeen-year-old with a silly haircut, blank expression, and inflated sense of his own importance. He didn't know me from Adam Ant. Having extricated himself from his opponent's clutches, the great Sid Vicious simply marched past me and went on his merry (read: tired and emotional) way, to see the Ramones finish their set. He didn't even look at me, let alone pass judgment.

Disappointed? You bet I was.

The Pistols very quickly turned into caricatures, and they make a poor showing on my ATF (All Time Favorites) punk playlist. This is probably the most proscriptive playlist I've got, and contains everything from early Velvet Underground right up to the Hives. Opinions differ about the provenance of punk, although the counterblast really began on August 16, 1974, in front of a tiny crowd in a seedy New York City bar called CBGB, when four monosyllabic nerds from Queens walked onstage—Johnny, Joey, Dee Dee, and Tommy Ramone. Given they spent as much time shouting at each other as playing, the concert was a mess, but they improved rapidly, and it soon became clear they had hit on something.

Punk, basically.

Before them were the Velvet Underground (1966), the Stooges (1968), the MC5 (1969), Jonathan Richman (the first Modern Lovers album was recorded in 1973 even though it wasn't released until four years later), Richard Hell ("Blank Generation" was written in 1974), and then Patti Smith, with *Horses* (1975). The Ramones' first album was released in 1976, swiftly followed by the Damned's "New Rose" (November 1976), the Sex Pistols' "Anarchy in the UK" (November 1976), the Buzzcocks' "Spiral Scratch" (January 1977), and the Clash's "White Riot" (March 1977). The lineage then continues all the way through the Jam, ATV, the Stranglers, Television, and the rest and right up to the release of the belated Siouxsie and the Banshees single "Hong Kong Garden" (which to these ears always sounded like an adrenalized advertisement for a particularly enterprising Chinese takeaway) in August 1978. Punk then begat new wave, which begat power pop, which begat mod (pathetic!), 2-Tone (genius!), electropop, and the cult with no name (which is what Spandau Ballet and Culture Club were called before they became new romantics).

By the end of the decade punk had fizzled out, leaving in its wake a new generation of acts whose thirst for success far outweighed any absentminded idealism (it was fitting that the first British number-one single of the 1980s was "Brass in Pocket" by the Pretenders). Anyway, my punk playlist has 216 songs on it, and is by no means complete but includes the Clash, the Buzzcocks, Generation X, Thomas Leer, Ian Dury, Spherical Objects, the Slits, and everything from the Undertones to the Gang of Four and from X-ray Spex to 999 (I know they were crap but "Emergency" is still one of my favorite records). The big problem with punk is that not all of it sounds that wonderful anymore. Extraordinarily exciting and almost visceral at the time (the opening chords of the Clash's "Complete Control" are probably the most electrifying moments ever committed to vinyl, a call to arms that has only increased in stature over the years), much of it now sounds compartmentalized, almost as though it exists only in a time capsule. Out of context stuff like ATV, Chelsea, the Damned, and the Saints—even a lot of the Jam, come to that—sounds tinny and dated. And when you've got people like the Hives and the Libertines and the Strokes and Franz Ferdinand making punk with twenty-first-century production techniques as well as a twenty-first-century sensibility (tempered, knowing, smart), they make a lot of late-1970s punk sound old-fashioned and ill-considered. Music we hear when we're a teenager tends to define us for life, and although we might think that the stuff made when we were that age surpasses anything that came after it (or before it), these days people think exactly the same, claiming "old" pop—i.e., the stuff made in the 1960s and 1970s—sounds "unfinished." (To my ears Queens of the Stone Age don't sound better than Led Zeppelin, but to a lot of people they do, and why not?)

I loved punk when I was sixteen, and at the time probably felt more passionately about it than I have ever felt about anything in my life. I dressed like a punk, bought punk records—hundreds of the damn things—and went to dozens and dozens of gigs (the Damned and the Jam at the 100 Club, Elvis Costello and the Attractions at the Nag's Head in High Wycombe, the Stranglers at the Rainbow, the Clash at the Rock Against Racism concert in London's Victoria Park, the Ramones at Aylesbury Friars, the Buzzcocks at the Hammersmith Odeon, Chelsea, Generation X, X-ray Spex, Public Image, the lot, but I can't listen to a lot of it these days, as it grates too much. It reminds me of tower blocks, being beaten up on the night bus, walking six miles home, having beer for breakfast and chips for tea. A lot of punk reminds me of being poor, being a student, being an outcast. Punk produced some of the best music in the world, music that, from mid-1976 to early 1979, reinvented itself every five minutes, and yet . . . and yet, the sky is black, the speed is cut, all the girls have peroxide hair, and everyone disguises their accent.

Having moved to London, I quickly became obsessed with it, became obsessed with finding out where everything was, how everything linked together (how did you get from Sloane Square to the Holloway Road?), where everyone lived (John Lydon lived in Chelsea, I'd read, but where exactly?) . . . I wanted to know everything about everywhere. Why was East Ham miles away from West Hampstead? Why wasn't Stamford Hill really a hill? Where exactly was Abbey Road? (I was one of those thousands of Bowie freaks who needed to know where the cover of *Ziggy Stardust* was shot, and, after living in London for a few months, discovered it was done on Heddon Street, just off Regent Street.) Where were all those places that Ian Dury talked about? How could you really come to grips with punk unless you knew all the references, unless you knew what Billericay Dickie was all about?

London has been eulogized in books, in plays, films, poems, and, not least, in songs. But the city has no real anthem, nothing to compare with Frank Sinatra's "New York, New York," few things as evocative as "Paris in the Spring" or Dean Martin's "Napoli." Songs about London are not usually moments of epiphany; they tend to be colloquial, sentimental, cozy—sort of British.

During the late nineteenth century, music hall gave rise to many London songs such as "Burlington Bertie from Bow" and "If It Wasn't for the 'Ouses in Between"; in fact most eulogies to London have a music hall quality about them, from "Maybe It's Because I'm a Londoner" right through to "Up the Junction" (Squeeze). There have been others, songs like "A Nightingale Sang in Berkeley Square" (from the 1920s), Noel Coward's "London Pride" (popular during the Blitz), "Chim Chim Cheree" and "Portobello Road" (both from Disney films), and of course the appalling "Streets of London" by Ralph McTell. But by and large it has been left to pop music to supply the soundtrack to the city.

During the late 1950s London was a magnet for burgeoning pop stars, and Soho coffee bars like the 2Is, the House of Sam Widges, the Heaven & Hell, and Le Macabre became the focus of British pop culture. But few decent London songs emerged from the era. By the early 1960s the success of the Beatles and Merseybeat had shifted attention from London so much that groups from the south would pretend to be Liverpudlian in order to attract record-company attention.

The Kinks changed all that.

More so than the Beatles, the Stones, or the Who, the Kinks have an enduring association with the capital. Ray Davies, the group's songwriter, spent his formative years in Muswell Hill, and many of the band's songs were set in the city, among them "Dedicated Follower of Fashion" (which I think should still be played in every "quirky" little Japanese jeans shop in Soho or NoLiTa), "Berkeley Mews," "Willesden Green," the 1971 LP *Muswell Hillbillies* (the cover of which shows the band drinking in the Archway Tavern, Holloway), "See My Friends," and of course the classic "Waterloo Sunset"—which some would say is the quintessential London record and a song to rival "Lullaby of Birdland" or "Under the Bridges of Paris" for evocative mood and power. Davies wrote the song in memory of the time he spent in St.

Thomas's Hospital opposite the Houses of Parliament as a youth. "Two nurses wheeled me out on to the balcony, where I could see the Thames. It was just a very poetic moment for me. Ever since it's [been] my centre."

And then there was "Swinging London," those few brief years in the mid-1960s when London was the most fashionable place in the world; all of a sudden the capital had attitude. And there were songs too: "Itchycoo Park" by the Small Faces, "Play with Fire" by the Rolling Stones, "The London Boys" by David Bowie. Inevitably there was also some extraordinary bandwagon-jumping, this time by the likes of Roger Miller ("England Swings") and the New Vaudeville Band ("Finchley Central").

London next became a focus for pop during punk's heyday. The cult was born in London and the city became a metaphor for the whole movement: urban decay, anarchic fashion, backstreet violence, fast drugs, silly hair. The town became vaguely mythical, a magnet for the future punk royalty: the Jam's Paul Weller was so obsessed with the city he would travel from Woking up to the West End just to record the traffic (one of the band's earliest songs was called "Sounds from the Street," and their first two albums are so poorly produced they don't sound much better than Oxford Circus at rush hour). The group's urban fixation showed in "Down in the Tube Station at Midnight," "In the City," "A Bomb in Wardour Street," and bassist Bruce Foxton's dreadful "London Traffic" (" . . . going nowhere"—nice one, Bruce!)—all little snapshots of tough city life. Pop has always needed the city's shroud to make it cool—how could you be a market-town punk or an East Anglian mod? One of punk's defining rationales was reinvention; when we arrived in London, none of us wanted to admit we had actually been brought up in Henley or Swindon. And Woking? Puh-lease . . .

The Clash also made a point of writing about London, often writing about little else, although they tended to concentrate on Notting Hill and all points west. Pop archaeologist Jon Savage once called *The Clash* "virtually a concept album about North Kensington and Ladbroke Grove," containing "White Riot," "London's Burning," "48 Hours," and all the rest. While they soon cast their concerned eyes over the Middle East, South America, and any imploding quasi-Stalinist state they could find, for a while London was their world, inspiring their two finest songs: "White Man in Hammersmith Palais" and, of course, "London Calling" (about which Joe Strummer said, "I want it to sound like it's coming through fog over the Thames").

Punk's Gilberts and Sullivans couldn't leave the place alone, and every one of them—Ian Dury, Elvis Costello, Jimmy Pursey, and whoever wrote the songs in Chelsea, Bethnal, London, and 999—felt they had to say *something* about the damn place.

Then came Madness. Most good pop has an air of melancholy about it, and Madness's paeans to north London are no exception. "Our House," "Grey Day," and "Cardiac Arrest," in fact most of their songs, evoke the pathos and bathos of small lives in the big city. Their songs are both euphoric and maudlin, odd little tales of woe spilling out of Camden Town, the backstreets of Somerstown, and the fields of Hampstead Heath. Madness were the consummate colloquial pop group, and their London is full of gray skies and Routemaster buses, small-time crooks and barstool philosophers. Sharp-witted, eccentric, and often staggeringly blunt, their songs are much like Londoners themselves.

The West End became trendy again in the mid-1980s, when the rejuvenation and gentrification of Soho coincided with style culture's obsession with the pop mythology of the 1950s and 1960s. This culminated in *Absolute Beginners*, Julien Temple's fairly awful attempt at re-creating the Soho of hipsters, beatniks, and cappuccino kids. Elsewhere this relentless pursuit of a mythical postcode manifested itself in coffee bars, style magazines, nightclubs . . . and hardly any good songs about London. The one group to wring anything out of this period were a long-forgotten band called Boys Wonder, who wrote the occasional great London song but who never had a hit—in itself the perfect metaphor for the time. The only truly great London song from the 1980s remains the Pet Shop Boys' "West End Girls." (Ironically, the best song to celebrate the town as the after-dark glamour capital of the world, one full of poor people pretending to be rich and rich people pretending to be poor, is Roxy Music's "Street Life," made in 1973, when London wasn't especially cool at all.)

Faux cockney has been the hip lingua franca of British pop for half a century, exploited by stars like David Bowie, Cockney Rebel's Steve Harley, and Suede's Brett Anderson (not to mention Dame Mick Jagger, whose implausibly theatrical cock-er-ney drawl remains one of the greatest inventions of the late twentieth century). But during the Britpop years (roughly 1994 to '96) mockney's finest exponent was Blur's Damon Albarn, whose professional slumming involved professing a penchant for greyhound racing and fairgrounds. And while most people's fondest memories of the period are probably bound up in Oasis's "Wonderwall," Albarn's "Parklife"—the ultimate tongue-in-cheek celebration of London lad culture—is the defining record of the time.

Today's esturial emperor is the Streets' Mike Skinner, the street poet laureate who is justly celebrated from Elephant & Castle to Seattle, although the world that Skinner celebrates—a chavster's world full of blow, booze, Sky TV, mobiles, and fast food—is one found in every city in Britain, not just London.

Perhaps the reasons there are so few songs written about the metropolis anymore are because *(a)* there is no single homogenous image of the city, and *(b)* all the old images are redundant clichés. London today is just another urban sprawl, a Dickensian theme park without its own culture, a city full of fragmented communities and dozens of Starbucks, much like any other Western city. For years the only music coming out of the city that has had a sense of locality has been rap, but dance music is now so global it seems old-fashioned to sing about old London Town.

So I guess unless you're happy to include Ralph McTell on your playlist, then the city's anthem is "London Calling."

7

Steve Jobs Approximately

It's Steve Jobs, not me, who's in love with Bob Dylan

The land of Apple lies fifty miles south of San Francisco, in Cupertino, at the southern end of the bay, smack bang in the middle of Silicon Valley. The company arrived here in the late seventies and has remained in the same lush location through all its ups and downs, through all its trials, tribulations, and changes of CEO. It's now spread over dozens of buildings off De Anza Boulevard, not far from where Steve Jobs went to school. The town is home to sixty high-tech companies, including Hewlett-Packard, IBM, and Sun Microsystems.

The entrance to the Apple HQ bears a simple nameplate: "Infinite Loop," along with a colossal Apple logo, a logo— *the* logo, now one of the most recognized in the world—that is echoed throughout the complex, appearing on everything from door handles to notepaper. Its design, which will always be indebted to the Beatles, no matter what, is now nearly as identifiable as those belonging to Coca-Cola, McDonald's, and Nike, the holy trinity of internationally recognizable symbols, part of the everyday landscape of popular consumerism, and one of the few brands that can be identified solely by its logo. Jean-Louis Gassee, who founded Apple France before moving to Cupertino as chief technical wizard, thinks the logo is one of the defining symbols of its age: "You have the apple—the symbol of knowledge. It is bitten—the symbol of desire. You have the rainbow—but the colors are in the wrong order. Knowledge, lust, hope, and anarchy: any company with all that cannot help being mythic."

Infinite Loop is a seriously impressive corporate center, a sprawling, multi-acre site with beautifully manicured lawns featuring enormous pixilated sculptures, a gym, and one of the most amazing cafeterias in California: chef-prepared salads, a sushi bar, made-to-order wood-fired pizzas, a pasta counter, salad desk, burrito counter, smoothies, the lot. Smoking is not allowed anywhere on Apple property, not even away from the buildings.

Years ago, in the early 1980s, when the computer industry was really still in its infancy, there was no reason to be ostentatious—in fact it was detrimental. If you wanted to convince customers and investors that you were a lean, thrifty outfit, you had to appear that way. But not anymore. Nowadays, unless you have a vaulted ceiling, a glass atrium, or an I. M. Pei conservatory then you're really nothing. (In a eulogy to his former company, and with the deftness of a corporate publicist, ex-Apple CEO John Sculley said, "Everything at Apple is as much about perception as reality.") With its green-glass windows and curved metal atrium, Infinite Loop feels like any other eighties-inspired postmodern office block that has dared itself to be different, and its strict geometries of stone and glass feel as conventional as a Doric column. It is certainly not Silicon Valley's finest architectural achievement, and looks as though it should house an advertising agency that specializes in corporate affairs. But it is grand. And the difference here is security. There is a lot of it.

Apple's research and development facilities are some of the most secure buildings on the Apple campus. Here, shredding machines are considered old hat, and confidential papers (which these days are usually printed e-mails) are discarded into locked waste-paper baskets that are emptied at least twice a day. There are guards on every corner, while the electronic ID badges worn by the staff are used to monitor personnel movement as well as to simply allow entry to restricted areas.

This has less to do with corporate paranoia and more to do with the fact that industrial espionage in the technology industry is as rife today as it used to be in the secret services. Because of this, and because Apple is the sort of company that enjoys stuff like this, new products and processes tend to be known internally by code words. These are usually coined by the engineers and designers responsible for producing them, although there are certain trends that are popular. First came girls' names (rather unimaginatively named after girlfriends, wives, offspring, etc.), then fruit (as well as the Macintosh variety of apple, Pippin and Jonathan were also popular), and more recently the sort of ironic retroperceptive names that litter the Pixar movies (the original five colored iMacs were known know in both internally and externally as Life Savers). Others include Smeagol (Mac OS X 10.2.7), Jackson Pollack (QuickDraw), Gelato (the Newton MessagePad came in two flavors, 1 MB and 2 MB), Onyx (PowerBook G4), etc. As far as anyone can remember, the iPod was always just known as that.

Engineering miracles are an everyday occurrence here.

Jonathan Ive works in a huge open studio containing a number of communal design areas. A certain amount of transparency is required here, as it is at other high-tech companies (Nike, up in Portland, Oregon, springs to mind). The rationale effectively means that if your rank allows you to walk through glass, then you should be allowed to see everything on the other side. Here, everyone can see what everyone else is doing. "We have little exclusively personal space," says Ive. "In fact, the memory of how we work will endure beyond the products of our work." The physical environment reflects and enables the collaborative process. "We have assembled a heavenly design team," Ive continues. "By keeping the core team small and investing significantly in tools and process, we can work with a level of collaboration that seems particularly rare."

Apple's design guru is obsessed with music—liking everything from ironic nu-metal to computer-generated chillout—and he's proud that the design workshop possesses by far the loudest sound system on the Apple campus, a sound system fed by his iPod. "If I hadn't made it," he says, "I would have bought one as soon as I'd understood what it was."

The designers in the workshop are an eclectic bunch, and come from all over: the U.K., Japan, Australia, New Zealand, and—of course—California. Most of them have been together for more than a decade, and Ive still calls them his closest friends. He likes to say that what they share is the ability to look at old objects anew, even if it's something they use every day, or even something that they've designed themselves.

This is where Jonathan Ive sends his e-mails to Sir Paul

Smith in London. The fashion designer is one of the first people Ive sought out when he moved to California in the early
nineties, even though Paul lives in London's Holland Park.

"He was visiting London and just rang up and asked to
see me," Smith tells me, in his Covent Garden HQ. "I think
he thought I was one of the few people who could understand what he was trying to do at Apple. And I was. When
we eventually met we just devoured each other. We've met
dozens of times since, and whenever we have supper, we'll
talk about the joys of aluminium or the fiber of a particular
sort of plastic. I remember once we were in this restaurant in
Tokyo with some of his team, and we spent the evening discussing the relationship between the paving stones outside
and the wooden door frame of the entrance."

Smith is Ive's designer soul mate, and having happened
upon someone who shared the same design values, who had
the same passions and excitements, Ive sent him one of the
first iPod prototypes.

"One morning this . . . box arrived, and in it was this
pod-type thing. I didn't know what it was, I thought it was
some sort of new minidisc or something, and to be honest
with you, it stayed in its box for nearly a week until I could
get round to working out exactly what it was and what it
did."

But when he did finally get it working, Smith was hooked,
and over the space of a few weeks got various members of
his staff to upload his vast CD collection onto it (everything
from Van Morrison, U2, and Björk to—nowadays—the
White Stripes, Franz Ferdinand, and Coldplay). He was the
proverbial early adopter. Since then Smith has received
dozens of food parcels from Ive, and just an hour before I

spoke with him had taken receipt of a brand-new twenty-inch G5 iMac, one of the first in the U.K. It came with a handwritten note from Ive, signed "Jony."

"I think Jonathan and his team are just the best designers there are, and talking to them about design is like talking to Paul Weller about fabric—they totally know what they're talking about. They all have this incredibly boyish enthusiasm. And as for the iPod, it's just the most amazing piece of kit there is. It just feels so good in your hand—it's so ergonomic. I love the wheel, as it's basically a circular mouse. How clever is that! He sits all day in his office inventing stuff like this."

Formal gatherings at Infinite Loop, or at least the important ones, are always held in the boardroom, which is in the only high-rise building on Apple's low-slung campus. The long wooden table can seat up to three dozen people and allows a panoramic view of the expanse of Silicon Valley. This is where Jobs held court when he returned to Apple in the mid-nineties, asking his designers to bring him their "projects," to see what they were working on.

Jobs's office sits on the fourth floor, a room with a less-than-spectacular view of Silicon Valley than you might expect: you see the shrubby treetops extending out toward San Francisco Bay and the distant rush of the traffic on the freeway below. This is where Jobs comes when he isn't taking his corporate helicopter/baronial perk over to Pixar, across the Bay Bridge up the coast in Emeryville, or using his Gulfstream V jet (given to him by Apple when he accepted the role of CEO) to fly off to New York, L.A., or Europe. This is where he sits when he's pontificating on the reconfiguration of content delivery systems. When he is in this mood, Jobs is not just an evangelist for his company and his products; he is an evangelist for the whole notion of digital revolution. In the flesh Jobs is the same as he ever was: jeans, New Balance sneakers, and the trademark black polo-neck sweater. If he were a Simpsons character, he would be a trendy New Age priest, espousing the delights of digital technology as though it were a new religion.

This is also where Jobs is rumoured to tinker with a prototype 110 GB iPod, enough surely, to hold all of his beloved Bob Dylan collection. Jobs has been listening to Bob Dylan for almost all of his life. He is a Dylan freak. In his teens he obsessed over Dylan's lyrics, and he spent hours and hours deciphering them. In the early days of Apple, Jobs would play Dylan tunes on his guitar in his backyard while his mother, Clara, washed his baby nephew in the kitchen sink. He played the same songs when he took breaks from constructing the first Apple in the family garage, and would spend hours listening to bootleg Dylan recordings on his reel-to-reel tape player in his room (it was once noted by some wag that, such was fans' fascination with the singer, bootleg obsessives would be willing to buy a recording of Bob Dylan breathing heavily—which to some people is what he does anyway). And he once—wearing, incidentally, a double-breasted jacket and a bright red bow tie—quoted the entire second verse of "The Times They Are A-Changin'" at a 1984 shareholders meeting ("I'd like to begin by reading part of an old poem by Dylan, that's Bob Dylan . . ."). In later life Jobs actually dated Joan Baez, and it's been suggested by some that the only reason he did so is because she was famously Dylan's lover.

"Steve Wozniak turned me on to him," says Jobs. "I was probably . . . oh . . . maybe thirteen, fourteen. We ended up meeting this guy who had every bootleg tape in the world.

He was a guy that actually put out a newsletter on Dylan. He was really into it—his whole life was about Dylan. But he had the best bootlegs, even better stuff than you can get today that's been released. He had amazing stuff. And we had our room full of tapes of Bob Dylan that we copied.

"He was a very clear thinker and he was a poet. I think he wrote about what he saw and thought. The early stuff is very precise. But, as he matured, you had to unravel it a little bit. But once you did, it was just as clear as a bell. I was listening the other day to "Only a Pawn in Their Game" and that stuff's as good today as when he penned it."

One of Apple's first employees, Daniel Kottke, says, "That's how I became friends with Steve Jobs. We used to talk about Buddhist philosophy. I had no idea he was connected with Woz [Steve Wozniak] at the time. We just talked about transcendentalism and Buddhism and listened to Bob Dylan."

Jobs even created a piece of programming language software that he called Dylan (which stood for "dynamic language"). For months after its launch in May 1994, Bob Dylan sued Apple for trademark infringement, although they later settled out of court, with Apple obtaining the rights to use his name. "It is our intention to license the Dylan trademark to any implementation which passes a standard test suite," said Apple's press release, somewhat pompously. The software didn't set the computer world alight, although Apple continued to use Dylan's name, even using the singer's image in its Emmy Award–winning 1997 "Think Different" ad campaign. For this they appropriated images of icons like Dylan, Einstein, Gandhi, and John Lennon and Yoko Ono. "Here's to the misfits, the rebels, the troublemakers . . . While some may see them as the crazy ones, we see genius." Jobs personally called Dylan and Ono at home to ask to use their image. He wanted to emulate the success of Nike's "Just Do It" and to a certain extent he did.

Dylan is one of the best-represented artists on iTunes, and there are fifty-one of his albums available for download, including two versions of his *Biograph* compilation and three "exclusive" tracks. At the launch of iTunes in the United States, Jobs demonstrated building a playlist beginning with "Simple Twist of Fate" and also showed how you could view videos, using Dylan's "Tangled up in Blue." Like the rest of us, Jobs believes *Blood on the Tracks* to be Bob's finest work. Until recently he thought his hero hadn't done anything of worth since then. When a *Business Week* journalist tried to turn him on to *Empire Burlesque* in the mideighties, Jobs asked the record to be taken off after the first song, reiterating his negative opinion of recent Dylan.

"As I grew up, I learned the lyrics to all his songs and watched him never stand still. If you look at the artists, if they get really good, it always occurs to them at some point that they can do this one thing for the rest of their lives, and they can be really successful to the outside world but not really be successful to themselves. That's the moment that an artist really decides who he or she is. If they keep on risking failure, they're still artists. Dylan and Picasso were always risking failure. This Apple thing is that way for me . . . If I try my best and fail, well, I tried my best."

Steve Jobs's adventures in the music industry have had a profound effect on his relationship with music in general and with his iPod in particular. Posing with Sheryl Crow for an article in *Fortune* in 2003, he said to the singer that he had never really understood the relevance of rap. But while mucking about with a prototype of the iTunes Music Store on his Mac, he began to download some of Eminem's tracks.

"You know, he really is a great poet," Crow said.

To which Jobs replied, "Yeah, he's starting to grow on me."

8

Yowsah Yowsah Yowsah:
Disco, Soul, & Sex!

Oh yes, lots and lots of sex . . .

I spent much of my teenage years pretending to be someone else. Dressing up is a particularly British affliction, and, on discovering punk at the tender age of sixteen, I was similarly afflicted. Like the Edwardians who roamed north London council estates in the late 1940s, the teddy boys who donned brothel-creepers and drape suits in the 1950s, or the mods of the 1960s with their mohair jackets and loafers, for me the 1970s was a decade of fancy dress.

I arrived in London in 1977 at the height of punk, fresh from school, wide-eyed and penniless (with billowing trousers and cheesecloth shirts), to start an arts foundation course at Chelsea School of Art, only to find a city awash with not so much musical anarchy as fashion insurrection; in short, style wars.

It wasn't the fact that London was full of punks that surprised me—it was the fact that everyone at my art school seemed to think that life was one big coming-out party.

There was a smattering of punks and hippies, of course, but there were also urban paratroopers, flame-haired girls masquerading as Rita Hayworth or Clara Bow, and half a dozen young turks trying to look like Bryan Ferry. Narcissism plumbed new depths as haircuts reached new heights; everyone had an alias, an ambition, and an aerodynamic coiffure to match.

Like a lot of people from my generation who came to London in the late seventies, it was reinvention I was looking for. I was also looking for fun, an education, and a career, but fundamentally I wanted to escape my past. "Everyone will hate you when you grow up because you're middle class," said my mother when I was about fourteen. 'The upper class will hate you because you're encroaching upon them; the working class will hate you because you're trying to leave them behind; and the middle class will hate you because they see themselves in you, and don't want to be reminded of where they came from." Thanks, Mum. The subtext was always, "Deal with it."

Having spent a year at Chelsea School of Art, in the summer of 1978 I applied to St. Martins, the crucible of sex, art, fashion, and music, to study photography and graphic design. What could be more fun? An art school in the middle of Soho! The center of the known universe! And although St. Martins was the first place the Sex Pistols played, supporting Bazooka Joe in 1975, it was already experiencing another sea change. It was in 1978 that the eighties first arrived, and they arrived first at St. Martins.

Being at art school in the late 1970s meant living in a playpen, a pop-cultural whirlpool of nightclubs, gigs, and parties, a world where punks mixed with public schoolboys, where soul boys danced with drag queens, where barrow boys dressed up to look like wing commanders. I'd only been there for five minutes before I realized I could be anyone! I didn't need to just dress like a punk, I could look like a pirate, a cocktail barman, a 1940s torch singer, a stevedore, anyone.

In many ways the late 1970s was the period when style culture really began to blossom in this country, when a generation of socially mobile boys and girls first began to understand—en masse—that their aspirations could be realized by simply looking the part. It was also the dawn of what became the New Romantic movement, when sartorial elegance became the easiest way to make your way in the world. And like many of my peers, it was a time when I changed my look at the drop of a wide-band trilby; one minute we were Lower East Side punks in plastic leather jackets and baseball boots; the next we were Soho secret agents, stalking moodily around West Wonderland in cheap raincoats and floppy fringes—a different haircut for every day of the week.

During the late seventies and early eighties there were occasions when I suppose I would admit to being a fashion victim, but then I always hated myself in the morning. There were, though, lots and lots of those mornings. And evenings too; evenings when I wore my black velvet bomber jacket with a fake-fur collar. Then there was the three-quarter-length two-piece Prince of Wales checked drape suit made for me by a little man in Harrow (which I first wore, if I remember rightly, to the Bri-Nylon retrospective at the V&A).

And how can I forget my "Hard Times" distressed jeans, which, by the time I was finished with them, had more holes than a decent Emmental and smelled like one too? My own particular favorite was my "punk matelot" look: motorcycle jacket, striped T-shirt, earring, white navy fatigues, and winkle-pickers—with hindsight I must have looked like a Latin American rent boy.

Style culture in those days was rather a clandestine endeavour; groups of friends thought and looked alike, giddy in the knowledge that they—we—were somehow different from the crowd. These days style culture is all pervasive; it surrounds us like the air we breathe, but back than it was elitist in the extreme.

On Charing Cross Road there was pub called the Cambridge, just a Sid Vicious spit from St. Martins, and the trendiest bar in all London, whose upstairs bar was always full of art students, former punks, pop stars, and fashion designers. Malcolm McLaren had his own stool, the Sex Pistols seemed to be there every Friday night, and Siouxsie and the Banshees took up residency by the jukebox. Jamie Reid was the coolest man there. He designed everything for the Sex Pistols (the single sleeves, the posters, the ads), and to a seventeen-year-old graphics student was a genuine, 24-carat, bonafide hero. He always wore a tight, thigh-length black leather suit jacket, his hair was always fashioned into this greasy, truck-driver quiff, and he had a bottle of Pils seemingly grafted to his left hand. Pils was the only thing that anyone drank, making us think it was the only thing they sold.

Everything happened at the Cambridge: a girl was decapitated by a truck after she bet her friend she could crawl underneath it before it pulled away outside; a St. Martins fine art student called Alan was beaten senseless because he persisted in dressing like Hitler (floppy fringe, jackboots, leather trenchcoat, and telltale mustache). The first time we saw him, we immediately took bets on how long it would take before someone kicked the living daylights out of him. And just two weeks later he stumbled into the Cambridge covered in the most fearsome bruises. Alan had, to quote an old Nick Lowe song, been nutted by reality, and soon left the college.

Most people congregated at the Cambridge before moving off into the night, to the latest tranche of nightclubs sprouting up all over the city. With the fancy-dress parade at its height, a generation of young entrepreneurs was taking over nightclubs for one night a week, installing DJs and creating a phenomenon out of nothing. The only condition: you had to dress up. I lived in nightclubs for nine years solid, from 1979 to 1988, starting with the Blitz, St. Moritz and Hell, through Le Beat Route, Club for Heroes, the Wag Club, and the Camden Palace, right up to White Trash, Do-Dos, Café de Paris, and Taboo. These clubs were the breeding ground of the eighties, the clubs that produced a new generation of pop stars (Boy George, Spandau Ballet, Wham!), fashion designers (John Galliano, Katharine Hamnett, Bodymap), film stars (Tim Roth, Daniel Day-Lewis, Sadie Frost), journalists, photographers, designers, and the club entrepreneurs themselves, many of whom would go on to launch restaurants, hotels, and the like. These were not the discos of my youth, not the sweaty rugby clubs where we used to stick our thumbs in the pockets of our high-waisted trousers and headbang away to "Hi-Ho Silver Lining" and "Brown Sugar," not the youth clubs where, at the end of the evening, you'd find yourself with your arms around an inappropriate girl, smooching along to the Chi-Lites' "Have You Seen Her?" or 10cc's "I'm Not in Love." No, these places were somewhere else completely, serious dens of iniquity where the main preoccupations were fashion, sex, drugs . . . and dancing.

If there's one thing that helped turn me from a neurotic

boy outsider to a relatively gregarious grown-up, it was learning to dance. Really dance. My self-administered emancipation was found on the dance floors of nightclubs all over central London, dancing to the sort of music that, would, for a few years at least, become my alternative DNA.

After all the raw emotion and unsullied rock of the seventies, the eighties were all about cold conformity, unabashed ambition, and surface smarts, and all of it standardized by a metronomic backbeat. Essentially, dance music has always been driven by fashion and technology, so it's no surprise that much of it concerns itself with the notion of perfection, and variations thereof. As soon as drum machines began taking over dance in the mid-seventies, the art of the impossible became the only reason to make records: what exactly was the perfect beat? First we had click tracks, rhythm boxes (samba, mambo, bossa nova, etc.), and robotic synths; and then, in 1978 Roland launched the CR78 (famously heard three years later on Phil Collins's "In the Air Tonight"), and a year later Roger Linn launched the world's first mass-market drum machine. As soon as the Linn Drum appeared, it had a huge effect on the way records were put together, and for months afterward the charts were full of songs underscored by the metallic thud of the Linn Mark I. Drummers liked to say the sound was reminiscent of damp cardboard being struck by a large fish, although this prompts the question: how did they know? Roland then came up with the TR808 (heard on Marvin Gaye's "Sexual Healing"), then the 909, which was the drum box of Chicago house, and the TB303, the sound of acid house. Since then, digital recording equipment has become so advanced that all you need to make a record is a laptop and a bunch of bad ideas.

The three records that cartographically defined the start

of the new decade were "The Adventures of Grandmaster Flash on the Wheels of Steel" by Grandmaster Flash (Sugarhill, 1981), "The Message" by Grandmaster Flash and the Furious Five (Sugarhill, 1982), and "Last Night a DJ Saved My Life" by Indeep (Sound of New York, 1982). The first personified the scratching and sampling and stop-start techniques that would affect every record in some way for the next twenty-five years; the second was a forerunner of gangster rap and the whole culture of complaint; and the third was a coronation of the DJ as the axe hero of the eighties.

As soon as I descended into clubland, I began accumulating the best collection of disco records the world has ever seen. I bought them, danced to them, and then stuck them in boxes under the stairs. And then twenty years later I bought an iPod and they all came to life again. And they're all here, collated with love. There are 301 dance tracks on my "Ibiza" playlist, the oldest of which dates from 1971, while the most recent was uploaded about an hour ago. For the past fifteen years or so, dance has been embroiled in such a widespread and mediocre compilation frenzy that barely a week goes by without the release of another *Disco Fever* collection, usually featuring Kool & the Gang, Gloria Gaynor, and any number of badly remixed Bee Gees tracks. But that hasn't stopped the genre from developing its own "canon," an acknowledged litany of world-famous karaoke-friendly floor-fillers. And I own quite a few of them. In my meticulously created vacuum-sealed simulacrum of the best disco in town, these are the records you'll hear in the first hour or so, the twenty greatest "disco" songs in the world:

(1) "Don't Stop 'Til You Get Enough" by Michael Jackson (*Off the Wall*, Epic, 1979)

(2) "One More Time" by Daft Punk (*Discovery*, Virgin, 2001)

(3) "TSOP (The Sound of Philadelphia)" by MFSB (*The Sound of Philadelphia*, Philadelphia International, 1973)

(4) "Slave to the Rhythm" by Grace Jones (ZTT, 1985)

(5) "Music Sounds Better with You" by Stardust (Roule, 1998)

(6) "Lola's Theme" by Shapeshifters (Positiva, 2004)

(7) "Spacer" by Sheila and B. Devotion (Carrere, 1979)

(8) "Crazy in Love" by Beyoncé (*Dangerously in Love*, Columbia, 2003)

(9) "Shake Your Body (Down to the Ground)" by the Jacksons (Epic, 1978)

(10) "Going Back to My Roots" by Odyssey (RCA, 1981)

(11) "I Want Your Love" by Chic (Atlantic, 1978)

(12) "Lady" by Modjo (Polydor, 2000)

(13) "Let the Music Play" by Shannon (Warehouse, 1983)

(14) "Hey Ya!" by Outkast (*The Love Below*, Arista, 2003)

(15) "Rock Your Baby" by George McCrae (*Rock Your Baby*, Jay Boy, 1974)

(16) "Staying Alive" by the Bee Gees (*Saturday Night Fever*, RSO, 1977)

(17) "Hey Fellas" by Trouble Funk (Sugarhill, 1982)

(18) "Rock Your Body" by Justin Timberlake (*Justified*, BMG, 2002)

(19) "I Feel Love" by Donna Summer (GTO, 1977)

(20) "Trick Me" by Kelis (*Tasty*, Arista, 2003)

The best club music of the early eighties tended to be gay disco—Coffee's "Casanova," Lime's "Your Love," "I Can't

Take My Eyes off You" by the Boystown Gang, and any Hi-Energy record you care to mention. How could it not be? Dance music during this time was all about transgression and euphoria. Gay discos also tended to be where the most interesting people went after dark. Taboo was one such place, a Leicester Square nightclub that looked like the bar in *Star Wars*, full of weird, alien beats with intergalactic haircuts and tinfoil tunics. The woodwork squeaked, and out came the freaks. This is what I imagined the last days of Rome to be like, if the Romans had had discos, that is. Everyone dressed up, everyone danced, everyone had sex. Lots of sex. Fucking in the toilets, blow jobs at the bar, girls doing girls, boys doing boys, everyone doing each other. There was one infamous female journalist (who later turned into a quasi-pop star), who used to trade blowjobs for coke, and could regularly be seen traipsing off to the toilets accompanied by a boy with a hard-on and a rolled-up fiver. One night there, two famous fashion designers, one feted contemporary artist, and the lead singer of an enormously popular rock band were huddled together in a cubicle in the men's loo, hoovering up cocaine as though it was going out of fashion (fat chance). As they piled out, I overheard one of the designers say, to nobody in particular, "I do so much these days that when I go to the cashpoint [ATM] the notes come out ready rolled."

Sex was everywhere in those days. One night at Skin II (a fetish club you couldn't get into unless you were dressed head to cock in leather) I saw a bald-headed, leather-clad boy slowly push a big, black rubber dildo up a similarly bald, leather-clad girl's backside, as she bent lasciviously over the bar, quietly pleading with him to push it harder. This sight certainly kept me occupied while I waited for my beer. Another night I pushed open a cubicle door in Club for Heroes to find the lead singer of one of the most successful girl groups Britain has ever produced being taken from behind while she was throwing up into the bowl. She didn't seem to mind (nor did her bass player, who was snorting a line of coke on the windowsill). Everyone fucked themselves stupid.

As club culture began to get more sophisticated, or at least more homogenous, the records started to get more uniform. DJs would alter the bpm in order to slide seamlessly from one track to another, so that in effect what you got was one long song with various highs and lows. And as art tends to imitate life, so records started to get longer and longer—first five minutes, then six, seven, eight, then ten, then (unbelievably) sixteen or seventeen. In DJ booths the world over, the question was: how long can you keep it up for? In the laser-beamed, mirror-balled, smoked-mirrored eighties, the twelve-inch remix wasn't so much king, as it was an all-singing, all-dancing insomniac emperor with dancing feet, a propensity for fast drugs, and a libidinous streak as wide as the dance floor at Studio 54. Remixes started off as simple repagination, reassembling the constituent parts in a novel but comprehensible manner. Soon though, remixes were doubling in length, tripling, quadrupling. Patrick Cowley's 1982 remix of Donna Summer's "I Feel Love"—quite probably the most architecturally sound dance record ever constructed—is over fifteen minutes long, and for a while became the benchmark of dance remixes. It changed the way we played music at home too: I once played the SOS Band's "Just Be Good to Me" for over two hours. The three twelve-inch remixes I had were around eight minutes each, and I kept switching them around on my decks at home, the drums descending on my head like paving stones, the heavy-handed robotic synths marching forward with no particular place to go. It's an Amazonian record, as big and as sexy as you like—even today, when it's much easier to create songs on this scale—an absolutely compulsive piece of music from fanfare to finale. And making it longer only prolongs its licentiousness.

With digital technology, there's no reason why someone couldn't remix it so it's an hour long, a day long, or three and a half weeks long. Even with just a 40 GB iPod, Donna could be girding her loins for well over two weeks. And with Smart Playlists you can turn your playlist into one long seamless BPM-approximate soundtrack, an accompaniment that could see you through the whole night, from the early evening rush hour ("Does this cod-piece go with my tie?") to the two A.M. paparazzi stagger, when you're falling out of the cab. In fact, with my iPod my party can last for weeks, a never-ending one-night stand.

In a rather back-to-front fashion, disco made me treat soul music with more respect. Even though I had a boxful of soul singles from my early teens, by the age of twenty-one I thought I had moved on, thought that soul was for adolescent girls, not boys who desperately wanted to be trendy. But I came round quickly. After all, I soon realized that soul was the music of love. If twelve-inch remixes were one-night stands, then soul, and soul albums in particular, were full-fledged affairs. Soul music was fundamentally about love, L-U-V, about finding it, loving it, losing it, and missing it. That's what soul did best, and that's what you bought it for, especially if you were a man. If you'd broken up with your girlfriend, then it was perfectly OK to wallow in the soulful soliloquies you found on Motown or Atlantic. Shit, if Otis

Redding and Marvin Gaye were both man enough to say this stuff, then what was wrong with listening to it?

There are those who, in an attempt to keep soul music special and to distance it from the never-ending cycle of Motown/Atlantic/Stax/Kent/Northern Soul compilations, only champion the most esoteric, obscure stuff, but while I'm also sick of the now-ubiquitous Motown advertising jingles, I think there is an extremely fertile middle ground. And so, after careful consideration, I would volunteer the following as the twenty greatest soul songs of all time:

(1) "Ship Ahoy" by the O'Jays (*Ship Ahoy*, Philadelphia International, 1973)

(2) "All Day Music" by War (*Greatest Hits*, Island, 1976)

(3) "Sweet Soul Music" by Arthur Conley (Atlantic, 1967)

(4) "Joy and Pain" by Maze (MCA, 1981)

(5) "I'll Be Around" by the Spinners (Atlantic, 1973)

(6) "Fa-Fa-Fa-Fa-Fa (Sad Song)" by Otis Redding (Atlantic, 1966)

(7) "A Warm Summer Night" by Chic (*Risqué*, Atlantic, 1979)

(8) "Tired of Being Alone" by Al Green (*Al Green Gets Next to You*, Hi Records, 1971)

(9) "Me and Mrs. Jones" by Billy Paul (Philadelphia International, 1972), which was the first dance at my wedding in 1997

(10) "Ain't No Sunshine" by Bill Withers (CBS, 1971)

(11) "Be Thankful for What You Got" by William DeVaughn (Chelsea, 1974)

(12) "Why Can't We Live Together" by Timmy Thomas (EMI, 1972)

(13) "Harlem Shuffle" by Bob and Earl (OSE, 1963)

(14) "I Can't Stand the Rain" by Ann Peebles (Hi, 1973)

(15) "Dancing in the Street" by Martha Reeves and the Vandellas (Motown, 1964)

(16) "Don't Make Me Wait Too Long" by Roberta Flack and Donny Hathaway (*Roberta Flack Featuring Donny Hathaway*, Atlantic, 1979)

(17) "You Might Need Somebody" by Randy Crawford (*Now We May Begin*, Warner Bros., 1981)

(18) "Nights over Egypt" by the Jones Girls (*The Best of Philadelphia*, Philadelphia International, 1983)

(19) "Too High" by Stevie Wonder (*Innervisions*, Motown, 1973)

(20) "I'm Doin' Fine Now" by New York City (Epic, 1973)

It was also soul music that expedited the loss of my virginity, or plastic soul anyway. *Young Americans* is the album Davie Bowie made after finally ditching his Ziggy Stardust alter-ego, and all the variations thereafter (*Aladdin Sane*, *Diamond Dogs*, etc.), in an attempt at cracking the U.S. soul market. Recorded with such crack session musicians as guitarist Carlos Alomar and saxophonist David Sanborn, it's my favorite Bowie album, and remains his most underrated, full of heart-rending strings, searing sax, and enough minor chords to melt the coldest of cold hearts (even though he made it while on cocaine—one of the coldest of all drugs, it has an enduring warmth to it). Bowie calls it "plastic soul," "blue-eyed soul," and "the squashed remains of ethnic music as it survives in the age of muzak rock, written and sung by a white limey."

Unlike most people my age, dressing up wasn't just a

means to an end—it was a vocation. I didn't dress up to get sex; I dressed up to dress up. But they say that luck favors the prepared, and at the very tail end of 1977—when punk was at its height, nightclubs were eighteen months away, and the eighties were still choosing what clothes to wear—I had sex anyway. For the first time. We had been drinking in the upstairs bar at the Cambridge, and got talking as we were drinking up. We both lied about having a fondness for the Stranglers (who happened to be on the jukebox at the time—is there nothing people won't say in order to convince someone they're nice enough to have sex with?), walked down the Kings Road, and eventually to Ralph West (my place, not hers). I still maintain it was the clothes (mine, that is) that did it: a leather jacket (real this time) covered in punk button badges ("Blockhead," "Gabba Gabba Hey!" "If It Ain't Stiff It Ain't Worth a Fuck"), a black T-shirt, black leggings, baseball boots. And while I obviously know who was with me that night, I'm not certain she knows that she was responsible for dragging me (with hindsight, rather well) into manhood. In fact, given the extraordinarily comprehensive seduction techniques I displayed that night, I would imagine that she thought I had had sex, oh, exactly no times. But— and in the grand scheme of things, this is a pretty big *but*— while I can't truthfully recall what we were listening to while we were actually "doing it" (and we would have been listening to something, because that's what you did when you were seventeen), I have a fairly good idea that it would have been *Young Americans*. I say this because I would have probably put on side 1 the minute we got back to my room, and as we were listening to the title track, I would have poured two glasses of cheap white wine and spent rather too long ostentatiously rolling a joint on an LP sleeve (and the choice was always crucially important—I reckon at this juncture I would have used *Heroes* or my "Psycho Killer" twelve-inch), and then, just as the coagulating fug of intoxicants was beginning to envelop us, would have flipped the record over so we could both wallow in the luscious delights of "Somebody Up There Likes Me" and "Can You Hear Me" as the snow steadily fell over Battersea Park.

But I'm not sure. It could just as easily have been '77 or *Horses* or *The Idiot* or any number of Roxy Music albums I had lying around. Music to Seduce Women By is a whirling hosepipe of a subject (so to speak), and unless handled properly will flail about you, causing havoc and confusion as you inch your way along the sofa. When I was seventeen, the records I played whilst seducing a woman were simply a way of showing off, of proving I'd actually bought the new Blondie album or an Elvis Costello bootleg. As I got older, I became more cynical, and acquired a failsafe collection of CDs that were absolutely a means to an end: Marvin Gaye's *I Want You* (this is without question his best record, although for seduction purposes you should always try to skip the opening track, as you might come across as a little, er, forward), Ennio Morricone's *Once upon a Time in America*, Tom Waits and Crystal Gayle's *One from the Heart*, and any half decent Nick Drake compilation. In my experience, you don't really need more than three or four records because if she hasn't "bought it" (in the words of Woody Allen) by then, you may as well call her a cab.

Then, of course, there was always subject-specific targeting—using Simon and Garfunkel because you knew she liked them, and suggesting Depeche Mode for the same reason (although I'm not sure that any relationship based on a shared passion for Depeche Mode is destined to last, frankly).

Just as I was finishing the last paragraph I got a call from Alix in Paris, who happened to be playing Kool and the Gang through his iMac as he was finishing a piece for *Dazed and Confused*. When I told him what I was doing, he called me an amateur (par for the course, I'm afraid), and said that the best record for seducing women is Captain Beefheart's 1972 album *Clear Spot*, a record I only knew because one of its tracks, the willfully obtuse "Big Eyed Beans from Venus," was played on *The Old Grey Whistle Test* in the early 1970s and helped convince me that I should stop buying *Popswap* and start buying the *NME* immediately. Alix reckons it's the most romantic record ever made, and played me some of it over the phone. The three salient tracks are "Too Much Time," "My Head Is My Only House Unless It Rains," and "Her Eyes Are a Blue Million Miles," on which the Captain sounds like Otis Redding on acid, which is sort of how Beefheart sounded at the best of times, I suppose. He was infamous for corrupting the blues, although his unhinged "anti-music sound sculptures" were never commercially viable. Hence Doobie Brothers producer Ted Templeman, who was brought in to add some radio sheen to *Clear Spot*. It didn't trouble the charts of course, but the record was astonishing. But while Alix's choices are spot on, I think the object of your desire might question your intentions after listening to track 2, "Nowadays a Woman's Gotta Hit a Man," which, as a seduction tool, I think is right up there with Blink-182's "I Wanna F*** a Dog in the A$$."

In the pantheon of great lotharios, Captain Beefheart makes for an unlikely figure, although seduction is subjective territory, and one man's "Hot in Herre" is another's "My Ding-a-Ling." If I had the choice of taking tips from Nelly or Chuck Berry (who was famously arrested for secretly filming female guests using the toilets at his ranch), I would probably opt out and beg for Marvin Gaye, Prince, or Mick Jagger.

9

Digital Dreams: It's a CD!

Why Prince was the king of Swinging London

As a metaphor for the eighties, the CD is as good as any. Like Madonna, the Filofax, MTV, privatization, shoulder pads, and postmodern architecture, the CD is a defining symbol of the age, an age in which presentation was paramount. The compact disc compartmentalized its contents; cleaned them up, washed behind their ears, and then dressed them up for market; it digitally improved them, shrunk them, and then enshrined them in a pocked-sized jewel case. Like the designer decade it would soon become synonymous with, the CD was an emblem of burnished success—a smarter, more upmarket version of everything that had gone before it. The CD was new-school, cool. Not hip, not yet anyway, not totally, but certainly modern.

And the eighties were all about modernity . . . designer modernity.

Like Duran Duran, "designer" was big in the eighties. It became an adjective, applied to everything from vacuum cleaners (the Dyson) to pop groups (the Black Crowes being a designer Rolling Stones, for instance). From ad land's ideal home (Mont Blanc fountain pen, Braun calculator, Tizio lamp) to Tesco's fresh-food counter (Why buy radicchio rather than iceberg? Kos it says much more about you than ordinary lettuce can!), in the designer decade, design was everything and everything was design: designer deaths on your television screens, designer water next to designer beer in your fridge, designer labels in your wardrobe (lots and lots of those), designer condoms between your sheets, designer stubble on your face (worn by designer actors like Mickey Rourke and Bruce Willis).[4] And, how could we forget, designer sounds on the stereo. The CD was a designer product like no other, and heralded an era in which music became codified. Almost overnight, music became a lifestyle accessory, a background fizz to be played at designer dinner parties in designer lofts in designer postcodes. "CD music" became pejorative, as did the likes of Sade, Anita Baker, Dire Straits, and Simply Red. Critics said this was music with the edges rubbed off, with the soul extracted ("Crystal-clear sound for the couch potato generation!" they sneered). Aspirational in essence, if you didn't have the wherewithal to surround yourself with the occupational hazards of

[4]*Designer* was originally used adjectivally to describe the notionally elitist jeans produced by Murjani, Gloria Vanderbilt Jeans, in the seventies. It is said that the company wanted Jackie Onassis to lend the brand her name (and thus added value), but when it could not get the former first lady, it called in the New York socialite. The garments were advertised on the sides of buses with the slogan "The end justifies the jeans," alongside photos of a lineup of Vanderbilt-clad (signed) bottoms. *Designer* is now redundant as everything is designed: OutKast are the new Funkadelic; IKEA is the new MFI; the iPod is the designer Walkman.

yuppiedom—the waterfront conversion, the Breuer chairs, the cappuccino machine, the Golf GTi with the personalized number plate—then a few CDs left casually lying on the sub–Matthew Hilton coffee table would suffice. And whereas in the seventies we had rolled joints on LP sleeves, in the eighties our CDs were used for snorting cocaine. Simple as that. If, during the sixties and seventies, music was developed as revolution, in the eighties it was enjoyed as a lifestyle soundtrack.

It had a sound, the eighties, manifested in the Fairlight synthesizer, the Australian-manufactured machine used by Peter Gabriel, Thomas Dolby, Alan Parsons, Herbie Hancock, and *Miami Vice* producer Jan Hammer. If you wanted to sound futuristic, modern, then the Fairlight was your baby. And let's face it—at the time we all wanted to sound modern, whether we were pop stars or not. In the eighties, every established pop star from Bob Dylan to the Rolling Stones began using drum machines on their records, in the hope of being embraced by the new MTV Generation. Listen to anything from the eighties today—Madonna, Michael Jackson, Bon Jovi, the Eurythmics, Steve Winwood, the Pet Shop Boys, Sting—and you'll hear the time-capsule *clank* of overproduced synthesized drums.

For a while, all music on CD sounded like CD music, every track swathed in atmospheric synthesized swirls, every hook punctuated by piping sampled horns, and every crescendo building on banks of overlaid keyboards. And then there were the drums, the dreaded computerized drums. Music on CD sounded cleaner, leaner, less down and dirty. Initially it suited soul, heavily organized rock, and gentle singer-songwriter stuff, but wasn't so good at replicating the noise and squabble of punk or the energy and naïveté of rockabilly or early rock 'n' roll. And while digital recording technology offered the opportunity to add clarity to old recordings (sprucing up muddy recordings by everyone from the Shangri-Las to Sonny Boy Williamson with no scratches, clicks, or surface noise), it wasn't always suitable. Even the copying process felt impressively modern, clean, and computer-friendly. As the studio computer turned the music into separate binary codes—44,000 codes per second of sound!—you'd see the music in visual form, on a screen divided horizontally by bars (reflecting the frequency spectrum) with rising and falling levels following the bass, drums, guitar, vocals, etc. If you watched this for long, you'd begin to think you were living in some sort of perpetual Kraftwerk remix.

There are many records that defined the era, although not all of them stand up now (Tracy Chapman anyone? Erasure? Foreigner?). It was the decade when David Bowie (trying to please his fans) made his worst records, when the Stones (trying to please themselves) made their worst records; when Terence Trent D'Arby's debut LP *(Introducing the Hardline According to . . .)* spent eight weeks at number one, and the follow-up *(Neither Fish Nor Flesh)* died a designer death. Prince's 1987 opus, *Sign o' the Times*, was the best album of the eighties (the Clash's much lauded *London Calling* was actually released in 1979), a sexy smorgasbord of a record, the buffet at the porno-party of your dreams. It's all here: love, sex, religion, drugs, politics (sexual and otherwise), and a homemade sense of fun. It's a record that couldn't have been made in any other decade, layered as it is, with drum machines, samples, and modern studio wizardry. (It's the record that studio maverick Todd Rundgren would have made if he'd been born ten years later and knew how to dance.) And while it has the trademark studio sheen of any record made in the eighties, compositionally it is about as eclectic as it's possible to be and still retain a substantial fan base. Not only that, but Prince did everything himself: he wrote the songs, played most of the instruments, recorded and produced the record, and delivered the final product to the record company, who then distributed and marketed it.

Although he is American, Prince's entrepreneurial spirit was indicative of what was happening in Britain at the time. As society's safety net was swiftly reeled in and folded up, the pioneering spirit became the order of the day, and whether we went to work in banks or in nightclubs, going to work was what we tried to do. The eighties was the decade of dressing up and looking busy. All over the country the postpunk generation were dressing up to get ahead. Britain's obsession with youth culture seemed to intensify during the last few months of the seventies, and it was only natural that it would soon start to be reflected in the media. Up until that time our reading matter was principally American, and our perceived sense of style came from magazines such as *Interview, New York*, and the now defunct *Punk*. We might take a lead from something in the *New Musical Express*, or maybe *Tatler* or *Vogue*, but there was no magazine for us.

Until 1980, that is, when Nick Logan and Terry Jones started a small publishing revolution by launching, respectively, the *Face* and *i-D*. Logan, former editor of the phenomenally successful *NME* and creator of *Smash Hits*, and Jones, a former art director of *British Vogue*, both independently realized that style culture, or what was then simply known as "street style," was being ignored by much of the mainstream press. So they launched their own magazines, not only to catalog this new explosion of style but also to cater for it. The *Face* and *i-D*, which were aimed at both men and women, reflected not only our increasing appetite for street style and fashion but also for ancillary subjects such as movies, music, television, art, and zeitgeisty things in general—everything that was deemed to have some sort of influence on the emerging culture. They soon became style bibles, cutting-edge manuals of all that was deemed to be cool. Fashion, nightclubs, art, pop—if it clicked, it went in.

Pop music was vital in disseminating this new culture, and the emergence of the new pop groups such as Duran Duran, Frankie Goes to Hollywood, Eurythmics, Spandau Ballet, and Culture Club—who, in a move away from the punk ethos (more like a volte-face, actually), began spending their vast royalty checks in the designer boutiques along Bond Street and the King's Road—gave rise to a newfound tabloid interest in anything to do with pop.

Suddenly the red-tops latched onto the idea that pop was fashionable again. The lives and loves of Boy George, and Simon Le Bon, Annie Lennox, Holly Johnson, and the Kemp brothers, became front-page news. The pop stars believed their own publicity too, and many—particularly Duran Duran—began living the life of dilettantes and new-moneyed aristocrats, poncing about on boats and dating catwalk models. They had taken reinvention to its natural conclusion. Five years before their huge success, they had looked as though they were made of money even though their pockets were empty; now the good life was theirs for the taking. And they took it, each with both hands. Greed was good, after all, and credit so easy to come by, while dreams and wishes seemed so easily obtainable. In a way, success became democratized, and worlds that had once been available only to certain sets of people became accessible to, if not everyone, then at least anyone with enough luck and tenacity.

The pop world wasn't just fashionable—it was sexy too, and the arrival of androgynous celebrities such as Boy George and Annie Lennox put a whole new spin on Swinging London (British pop was then such a potent export commodity that in 1983 more than a third of all American chart places were taken by British acts). Pop stars began hanging out with fashion designers and frequenting the many nightclubs that were springing up all over the capital, PR agencies were beginning to exploit this newfound confluence of art and commerce, and the high street began taking notice of all the new money.

Affluence played an enormous part in the designer lifestyle boom of the early to mid-eighties, creating a divisive culture in which the yuppie dream was allowed to thrive. If you were on the right side of the fence, then the party went on all night.

In the mid-eighties, when style journalism hit its first peak, hedonism was de rigueur. I joined *i-D* magazine in the early eighties, and I soon realized that my social life was as important to my employers as what I actually did in the office. In fact, it was more important. It wasn't good enough to replicate the high points of Swinging London in the pages of the magazine, you actually had to live the life.

And live the life we did, in every nightclub and bar, at every ball and private view, 365 days a year. And usually for free (nobody paid for anything in those days). The mainstream media became so obsessed with the social habits of the five hundred or so "designer butterflies" who constituted the London scene that we were invited to everything. You went everywhere and you met everyone. These were the days when you'd bump into George Michael in the Wag Club dancing to his own records, or stand behind David Bowie in the queue for the men's room at the Mudd Club.

I remember one particular party, bizarrely enough in Harrods in 1985, where I was standing with a group of luminaries that included former Labour leader Neil Kinnock—slumming it for a bit of tabloid exposure—Duran Duran's Simon Le Bon, PR guru Lynne Franks, Boy George, fashion designers Jean Paul Gaultier and Katharine Hamnett, the American artist Julian Schnabel, and one of London's most notorious transsexual prostitutes. It was as if social boundaries had yet to be invented, as though social mobility was the birthright of anyone in a loud jacket and a pair of patent leather shoes.

Pop stars were everywhere, propping up the bars and piling into toilet cubicles. Walk into Club for Heroes, Heaven, or the Wag Club and you'd see someone from Spandau Ballet or Duran Duran, Madonna, Shane McGowan, Depeche Mode, August Darnell, the Pet Shop Boys, Boy George, Kirk Brandon, Pete Townshend, George Michael, and Andrew Ridgeley. (You went to Rio, Monte Carlo, New York, L.A., Tokyo, and Toronto, and they were all there too, propping up the bar and nodding as you walked in as though they were still drinking cocktails in Soho.) Wham!, a designer duo that exemplified controlled exuberance, personified the new decade. Suburban boys with West End aspirations, they were high street through and through, appealing to twelve-year-old girls, estate agents, and art students alike. They were also a welcome antidote to the hordes of shoe-gazers filling the pages of the music press. Who wanted to listen to some doleful Bolshevik ballad of oppression when you could be cutting a rug to "Club Tropicana"?

I first saw them in July 1983 at the launch of their debut LP, *Fantastic* (such confidence!), in a small suite of offices just behind the Fulham Broadway tube station. While dozens of sneering music journalists and record-company bigwigs stood about working at being brilliant, these two nineteen-year-old soul boys, dressed in Hawaiian shirts, cutaway jeans, and deck shoes, jived together on the dance floor, jitterbugging along to their own version of the Miracles' "Love Machine." Rarely had I seen two men enjoying themselves so much. To be dancing to one of their own records! At their own party! In front of other people!

After they became famous, they still went out, and it was not unusual to see Andy on display at the Limelight or George down at Taboo. For about eighteen months "Everything She Wants" (No. 2, December 1984) was the hippest record to be seen dancing to, and George could often be seen doing just that, right in front of the DJ booth. It was a common sight, yet still disconcerting, and while you might have shared a space at the bar and adjacent spots on the dance floor, there was George the next night, glistening with fame, on *Top of the Pops*. Even at three A.M. in the bowels of some sweaty West End nightclub (usually the Wag), dancing by himself to Phyllis Nelson's "Move Closer," he looked as though he'd just stepped off the plane from Ibiza: tandoori tan, summer whites, designer stubble (something he invented), and perfect Princess Diana hair: "Some days I made the covers of the tabloids. Some days Princess Di made the covers of the tabloids," he said. "Some days I think they just got us mixed up."

For a while Wham! and I even shared a tailor. From his shop in Kentish Town, an ex-boxer called Chris Ruocco would knock up suits and stage costumes for the boys, and you'd occasionally see them trying on a new pair of trousers, their hot hatchbacks double-parked outside. I once went for a fitting only to find Chris surrounded by thirty custom-built tartan suits, in readiness for the boys' upcoming tour of China. Needless to say, it was the Black Watch for me that summer.

It's possible to illustrate the mercenary tendencies of the decade by the simple fact that they were spent going to shop openings—not "happenings," not art events, and not always concerts. We collectively paid homage to consumerism. I went to thousands of parties in the eighties in many parts of the world, but oddly the ones I remember most took place in shops—the openings of Tower Records in Piccadilly, the Next store in Kensington, the Katharine Hamnett store in Brompton Cross, the HMV store on Oxford Street, the re-launch of Harvey Nichols, the relaunch of Way-In at Harrods, the opening of everything everywhere. And the thing that all these parties had in common was the fact that at each and every one of them I saw famous people thieving—walking off with magnums of champagne, CDs, jackets, bottle of perfume, silver trays full of uneaten canapés, other people's girlfriends. Everything was free in the eighties, even the things that weren't meant to be (*especially* the things that weren't meant to be).

During the eighties the media went fashion crazy as London became a crucible of self-expression, the center of anything and everything. Everyone wanted to buy into the dream, even pop stars. In 1986 I wrote a long and rather inflammatory piece in *i-D* about a silly Italian youth cult called the Paninari. In a style that now seems excited (actually, to be fair, it's a lot worse than that), I cataloged the Paninari obsession with casual sportswear, their predilection for riding little motorbikes through the streets of Milan and hanging out in sandwich bars (hence the name; a *panino* is a bread roll) and of course their reactionary prepubescent machismo. Acting on disinformation, I also wrote that the Pet Shop Boys—who were apparently big fans of Paninari fashion—had even recorded their own paean to the cult, called, simply enough, "Paninaro." When the song eventually appeared a few months later, I thought nothing of it. Until about three years later, that is, when I read an interview with the Pet Shop Boys in *Rolling Stone* magazine. They had read my piece: "We read that we'd recorded this song," said Pet Shop Boy Chris Lowe. "Of course we hadn't but we thought it was such a good idea that we soon did."

Style culture became the binding agent of all that was supposed to be cool. Catwalk models were no longer simply clotheshorses, they were rechristened supermodels. Fashion designers were no longer just considered gay iconoclasts or hatchet-faced prima donnas. They became solid-gold celebrities to be fawned over and profiled. Designers who had previously been demonized for their outrageous abuse of models and staff were now being sanitized for everyday consumption. Pop stars were no longer considered to be council-house Neanderthals but were suddenly elevated to front-page sex symbols, whose every word was copied down, amplified, and endlessly repeated in the gossip columns of the national press. It was a sartorial melting pot, a visual mélange of crushed-velvet miniskirts, high heels, and lipstick. And that was just the men.

In previous periods of intense fashionability in London—namely in the sixties, when class divisions in society first began breaking down—the consumer aspects were confined largely to the female market: trendy women's magazines, trendy women's shops, trendy female icons. But in the eighties it was different, and if the decade can be remembered for anything, it should be remembered as the decade in which the postindustrial man finally became liberated. If women found their sexual liberation in the sixties, then men discovered their social mobility in the eighties—as consumers.

The lifestyle explosion has reached saturation point. And as for street style, it doesn't really exist anymore. Doc Martens are no longer the boots of the disenfranchised but are worn by everyone from seventeen-year-old bricklayers to forty-five-year old architects, from schoolgirls to aging rock stars. Distressed leather jackets are just as likely to be found on the backs of advertising executives as they are on biker boys. People have done just about everything with their hair, with their clothes, and with their bodies, piercing all the parts it is possible to skewer.

As the American performer and comedian Sandra Bernhard said, there is not much more people can do to themselves "unless they start wearing lumber." Recycled nostalgia is now the thing, and in this postmodern age of arbitrary gesture and kitsch 'n' sink subculture, urban tribes are ten a penny.

Everyone's trendy now, everyone codified and hip to the modern world, while elitism is becoming increasingly fetishistic. Odd. Weird. Uncalled for. Why be willfully different when you can consume with impunity? For those of us who have come through the eighties unscathed and successfully negotiated the perilous contours of the new face of consumerism and the free-market economy, life is good. Very, very good indeed. And now many of us are the people we pretended to be all those years ago.

10

The Virtual Megastore:
Apple Launches iTunes

How Steve Jobs resuscitated the music industry

January 2001 was a big month for Steve Jobs. It was exactly a year since his keynote address at the Macworld Expo, the big comeback speech, the speech where Jobs finally drew a line in the cybersand. "I'm pleased to announce today that I'm dropping the 'interim' title," he somewhat flippantly stated, thus earning a standing ovation and confirming what many in the room had long thought: that since coming back to the company in 1997, Jobs would find it impossible to allow himself to leave again. After all, he had a job to do. Since the initial success of the iMac, the launch of the PowerMac G4 Cube had been greeted with a disinterested shrug by the industry, while Apple stock was taking a slow dive, along with most other companies associated with the dot-com bubble.

So the 2001 Macworld Expo was an important anniversary for Jobs, especially as he would be addressing his home crowd in San Francisco. It started well, however: not only did he unveil the supercool titanium-clad PowerBook G4 as well as the Mac OS X, he also announced the release—finally—of iTunes 1.0. At last, music software! Could this help the company move up through the gears? After twenty-five years, could music really be the answer to Apple's problems?

Ever since Jobs's return, Apple's "big idea" had been the iMac. But by the summer of 2000, just two years since the machine's debut, the company had sold 500,000 fewer iMacs than originally planned. The wine-gum-colored PCs were fast losing their novelty, although not for the reason many supposed (which was that the market was saturated). No, the problem was that Steve Jobs, a man not overly impressed by the dot-com craze, had missed one of the defining trends of the Internet generation: downloading. Many new computers had CD-RW ("read-write") drives that allowed users to burn CDs from the stuff they'd downloaded over the Net or fed in through their slot loaders. This was known in the trade as a "killer application," and was one Jobs had successfully ignored. By the end of 2000, over 40 percent of PCs had this function. But not one of them was built by Apple. Dell, yes; Hewlett-Packard, yes; even Compaq; but not the most innovative PC manufacturer of the age. As journalist and Apple critic Alan Deutschman wrote at the time, "Nearly 30 million PCs with CD-RW drives were sold in the year 2000, and none of them carried the Apple logo. It was ironic that Apple slapped the letter *i* next to the Mac to imply that it was an Internet computer when in reality Steve utterly ignored one of the Internet's hottest trends. Steve relied on his own instincts, but this was beyond his experience. Teenagers steal expensive things; billionaires don't have to." While iTunes 1.0 was a step in the right direction—as was the belated move of equipping Macs with CD-RW drives capable of burning audio discs, and updating Mac OS X to support this—but these steps merely put the Mac on equal footing with everyone else.

What could Jobs do to leapfrog his competitors? More important, did he realize he needed to?

Years ago, when I first began to experiment online, I found myself spending a small fortune on rare first editions from small independent booksellers in the wilds of Utah and Arizona. Having been a keen—some would say obsessive—collector of the works of Tom Wolfe since I was about thirteen, and having spent nearly thirty years pursuing his rarities through dealers and book searchers, the Internet made it possible for me to buy rare editions of his books at a fraction of what they usually cost. And, predictably, I got the bug (which is an addiction, as opposed to the computer bug, which was so named after a moth got trapped in one of the first mainframes). Soon, I was going online every afternoon, buying anything and everything I could get my fingers on—CDs I'd never find the time to play; books I'd owned and, having found them again, felt it would be churlish not to own again; videos and DVDs of impossible-to-get Japanese art-house movies (porn); old magazines; cushions; the whole kit and caboodle. I managed to find a copy of the first "grown-up" book I ever read (*Redcap*), the thousand-piece jigsaw of Alan Aldridge's famous Beatles poster, half a dozen rare Beach Boys CDs, the lot.[5]

---

[5]In my wallet I carry a piece of photocopy paper folded in eight. It contains a list of records and CDs I'm looking for, and usually has at least a hundred things on it. I've been keeping the list for about fifteen years, adding and deleting as I work my way through it. Some things I buy if I find them and they're cheap enough, some I

And then two things happened: first, I started to spend more on things from the Internet than I was spending on my own family; and second, I got burned (or at least Barclaycard did). After the credit card company took my word for it that I hadn't bought six internal flights in Belgium (are there six places worth visiting in Belgium?) or sixty-five secondhand luminescent phallic table lamps from a not entirely reputable wholesaler in Hamburg, I stopped buying online.

But then, something *else* happened. Something far, far more important. In a move that may well be remembered as a crucial turning point in the history of recorded music as well as the history of Apple, on April 28, 2003, Steve Jobs launched the iTunes Music Store, a revolutionary online venture that let customers quickly find, purchase, and then download music for 99 cents per song. And I wanted in. Other competitive online music services had been trying to "suck coin" out of the MP3 music craze but had failed to gain widespread popularity because they required paying subscription fees, had incredibly unsophisticated user interfaces, were restrictive about what you could do with your downloads, and offered only a small number of songs (oh, and in most cases, were totally illegal). With its seamless integration into iTunes 4.0, Apple's service was easy to use, and once you bought a 128-kbps AAC-encoded song, you were free to do almost anything you wanted with it: burn it to a CD, transfer it to your iPod, or listen to it on a Mac. Since Apple was able to obtain the cooperation of "the Big Five" music companies—BMG, EMI, Sony Music Entertainment, Universal, and Warner—the iTunes Music Store fea-

---

just look at in record shops knowing they'll still be there when I really want them, and some things I know I'll never find.

tured over two hundred thousand songs at its introduction, all of which could be previewed at the click of a button. Even though it was initially accessible only to Mac users, after a mere three months "on air," iTunes had sold over six million songs. And by the end of October, the number of songs available had doubled; not only that, but the Windows version was released, causing sales of e-songs to surge. After paying royalties and transaction fees, Apple earned only pennies per song, so it was easy to believe that the real motivation for creating the iTunes Music Store had been to sell more iPods, which carry significantly higher gross profit margins. "The iPod makes money. The iTunes Music Store doesn't," admitted Apple senior VP Philip Schiller. But even though Apple's strategy of using digital music as a Trojan horse to sell iPods was clearly working—it had sold over 1.5 million units in less than three years—in the process Steve Jobs had initiated one of the most important changes in the music business since the dawn of pop: he had legitimized downloading culture.

The record industry was changed forever in 1998, when Shawn Fanning, a teenage computer student from Massachusetts, launched a file-sharing network called Napster (his nickname). He was encouraged to start the site by his roommate, who complained incessantly about the slow links and out-of-date music available on the Internet. Fanning's genius software allowed anyone with an Internet-connected computer to share MP3 files; he initially gave a test version to thirty of his friends and asked them to pass it on. Which they did, with impunity. By May the following year, encouraged by the enormous response, Napster had over two million dollars of capital.

Six months later the Recording Industry Association of

America sued the company for copyright infringement, alleging that "Napster has created, and is operating, a haven for music piracy on an unprecedented scale . . . a giant online pirate bazaar." In June 2000 the RIAA got a temporary injunction to shut Napster down, although the court of appeals overturned the decision. Unsurprisingly, Fanning became something of a cult hero, and membership on the site shot through the roof, although it was finally closed down in July 2001, succumbing to the enormous legal onslaught. Then, in November 2003, after nearly two years in stasis, Napster was relaunched as a legal subscription service.

Of course Napster wasn't the only company offering music online, and during the early nineties there were hundreds of sites where you could find everything from old Pearl Jam tracks to Bob Dylan bootlegs—KaZaA, SoulSeek, Limewire, Gnutella, Morpheus, WinMX, dozens and dozens of the damn things. But not only did the recording industry begin clamping down on illegal users and lobbying for prosecution, artists got involved too: Metallica famously came out in favor of the record companies, and Madonna even made an MP3 of herself singing "What the fuck do you think you're doing?" and disguised it as a track on her new album and set it loose on the P2P world.

Unsurprisingly, there were just as many artists who thought the industry was being too uptight about the whole thing. "Imagine if book publishers decided they were against public libraries: Oh no, we don't like this because people can read books without paying for them and it's killing our sales," said David Byrne. "It's just not true. They might lose a tiny percentage, but they actually gain a lot more. When I was a kid you could check out LPs from the library, and that was file sharing. I discovered all kinds of experimental classic music and electronic music I never would have stumbled on if I had to go out and buy it because you couldn't buy it in Baltimore. The local stores didn't have those records."

Steve Jobs was bemused by the music industry's reluctance to satisfy the demand for Internet downloading that Napster had unleashed. After battering Napster to near-death in court, record companies had promised to launch paid services with the same limitless selection and ease of use. But they didn't, instead doing the polar opposite. Universal and Sony rolled out a joint venture called Pressplay. And AOL Time Warner (as it was, briefly, back then), Bertelsmann, EMI, and RealNetworks launched MusicNet. But instead of joining forces to attract customers, they competed to try and control the digital market, and refused to license songs to each other. Consequently neither service had enough songs to attract paying customers. Scared that downloading might cannibalize CD sales, these sites were subscription only; not only could you download MusicNet tunes onto just one computer, but they disappeared if you didn't pay your bill. "It was strictly the greed and arrogance of the majors that screwed things up," said Irving Azoff, manager of the Eagles and Christina Aguilera. "They wanted to control every step of the distribution process." Both companies eventually improved their services, but neither was as imaginative or as simple as iTunes, one of Jobs's very finest epiphanies.

Jobs didn't set out to be the music industry's savior, didn't intend to be its white knight, yet once he focused on music, he was consumed by it. How could it fail? He had the technology—he had the hardware, the software, and the distribution network—all he needed was the content. And the world was full of content providers, full of them! Why couldn't it work? After all, as André Breton said, the man who can't visualize a horse galloping on a tomato is an idiot. And this wasn't even about horses and tomatoes—it was really just common sense!

But when Jobs first approached record companies with a view to them getting onboard with iTunes, a lot of them were seriously skeptical.

"There's a lot of smart people at the music companies," said Jobs. "The problem is, they're not technology people. The good music companies do an amazing thing. They have people who can pick the person that's gonna be successful out of five thousand candidates. And there's not enough information to do that—it's an intuitive process. And the best music companies know how to do that with a reasonably high success rate.

"I think that's a good thing. The world needs more smart editorial these days. The problem is, is that has nothing to do with technology. And so when the Internet came along, and Napster came along, they didn't know what to make of it. A lot of these folks didn't use computers—weren't on e-mail, didn't really know what Napster was for a few years. They were pretty doggone slow to react. Matter of fact, they still haven't, in many ways. And so they're fairly vulnerable to people telling them technical solutions will work, when they won't."

Because, he said, of their total technological ignorance.

"When we first went to talk to these companies . . . we said, none of this technology that you're talking about's gonna work. We have Ph.D.s here that know the stuff cold, and we don't believe it's possible to protect digital content. It only takes one stolen copy to be on the Internet. And the way we expressed it to them is: pick one lock—open every door.

It only takes one person to pick a lock. Worst case: somebody just takes the analog outputs of their CD player and rerecords it—puts it on the Internet. You'll never stop that.

"At first they kicked us out. But we kept going back again and again. The first record company to really understand this stuff was Warner. They have some smart people there, and they said, 'We agree with you.' And next was Universal. Then we started making headway. And the reason we did, I think, is because we made predictions.

"We said these [music subscriptions] services that are out there now are going to fail. MusicNet's gonna fail, Pressplay's gonna fail. Here's why: people don't want to buy their music as a subscription. They bought 45s, then they bought LPs, then they bought cassettes, then they bought eight-tracks, then they bought CDs. They're going to want to buy downloads. People want to own their music. You don't want to rent your music—and then, one day, if you stop paying, all your music goes away.

"Nobody ever went out and asked users, 'Would you like to keep paying us every month for music that you thought you already bought?'" said Jobs. "The record companies got this crazy idea from some finance person looking at AOL, and then rubbing his hands together and saying, 'I'd sure like to get some of that recurring subscription revenue.'"

Even though Jobs was able to convince the Universals and the Warners of this world that iTunes was something to be embraced, they were not able to deliver all of their biggest artists, and so Jobs had to go to individual artists, one by one, and convince them to trust him. But he did it eventually, and succeeded in persuading the major record labels to stop fixating on their subscription models and take a radically different approach to selling music. Not only did iTunes commercialize online music sales, but also it clearly defined the previously hazy definition of what was legal and what wasn't. In 2003, the RIAA, the U.S. music industry's regulatory body, sued more than five thousand file sharers, and its tactics clearly worked: the number of people illegally downloading music files in the United States plummeted from twenty million in May 2003 to eleven million four months later. During 2004, the BPI, RIAA's U.K. counterpart, initiated a clampdown on illegal downloading that had an immediate effect on file sharing. There was also a drop in the number of people using peer-to-peer sites such as WinMx and KaZaA, and a rise in the number of people using the legal download sites, iTunes and Napster included. In January 2004 there were only 15,000 legal downloads a week in the U.K.; by September this was up to 160,000. And while Internet piracy was still rampant, as was CD piracy, the number of music files freely available online fell in 2004 to about 800 million from about 1.1 billion in 2003. By January 2005, over 6 percent of industry revenues were coming from legal downloads.

"It's kind of extraordinary that it wasn't a music company that cracked the problem of piracy," said Bono, adding that he thought it strange that music industry executives still refer to themselves as record industry executives when they "don't even make records anymore."

There is not yet a clear idea of what a successful business model for online music sales will look like. The problem for record companies continues to be that more people are buying single tracks rather than whole albums. And because those companies make more money when people spend, say, $12 on a single artist rather than $2 on six different ones, either the quality of albums will be improved (there is too much filler on CDs these days, even ones by major artists—*especially* ones by major artists), or the album as we know it will die. Because the majors were slow to embrace downloading, treating it as their nemesis rather than an opportunity, sales of recorded music shrank by a fifth between 1999 and 2003.

Perhaps the whole process of making music will spin off into other areas completely. John Peel's last discovery before he died was a band called Steveless, who went through a period of releasing an album every week (they're called Steveless, by the way, because there's no one in the band called Steve).

When the record industry first discovered Napster, it was tantamount to discovering that your wife was sleeping around—with every man on Earth who happened to own a computer. But since the success of iTunes, the potential of downloading became suddenly apparent. No longer would we walk into record shops, flick through the sleeves in the aisles, and make our selection; we would simply go online, browse, and then download like stink. And for the first time in two generations, the album was actually under threat as the primary means by which artists communicate with their audience.

Net tune competitors pop up hourly, but with iTunes' Windows rollout, Apple has 70 percent of the U.S. download market and sells four million songs worldwide a week. Even if some of that inevitably gets siphoned off, no one's likely to invent a product with more credibility than iTunes in Steve Jobs's (or Bill Gates's) lifetime.

"Apple's in a pretty interesting position," said Jobs. "Because, as you know, almost every song and CD is made on a Mac—it's recorded on a Mac, it's mixed on a Mac, the artwork's done on a Mac. Almost every artist I've met has an iPod, and most of the music execs now have iPods. And one of the reasons Apple was able to do what we did was because we are perceived by the music industry as the most creative technology company."

iPod a Spell on You

What are *the best records ever made?*

It's one-thirty in the morning and I've been at it for five hours. Having rushed home from work, I have been locked in the downstairs den since eight-thirty, gradually, methodically, pedantically working my way through my CD collection, uploading the chosen few onto iTunes, moving them into playlists as I go. For the past few days I've been working on "Ibiza," which is basically all sorts of dance music, from 1960s soul to twenty-first-century ready-mades; and "Sunland," which is one I made for my wife to be played on the Altec Lansing portable speakers on the weekends. "Sunland" is a fusion of West Coast early-1970s singer-songwriters (Jackson Browne, David Wiffen, Jimmy Webb, Dory Previn); loungecore classics ("Girl in a Sportscar" by Alan Hawkshaw, "Follow Your Bliss" by the B-52s, and "The Nearest Faraway Place" by the Beach Boys); lightweight supper jazz in the form of Grover Washington (a man I still think sounds like a hotel), Bobbi Humphries, Michael Franks, etc.; power pop; show tunes; ironic highway pop as produced by Phoenix, Air, and Corduroy; plus the odd bit of sunny-side-up Van Morrison and Coldplay. (Oh, and currently my three favorite records: "Everyone I Meet Is from California" by America, "It Never Rains in Southern California" by Albert Hammond, and "99 Miles from LA" by Art Garfunkel). There are 218 songs on this playlist and because of the Live Updating facility there will soon be many more. And so it goes on, ad nauseam, which is the point of the Pod.

I've just got into Smart Playlists too. The joy of Smart Playlists belies their ease of configuration. Just piece together a variety of criteria—artist, genre, rating, last played, etc.—and demand that iTunes create playlists based on songs that meet those conditions. So, for example you might want a Smart Playlist that includes only reggae songs you've never played, all uploaded on the AIFF format and all lasting more than seven minutes (unlikely, I know, but you get my drift). Alternatively you could configure the top row of your pop-up menu to read "Play Count is 0," and enable the Live Updating option. Select this playlist on your iPod and you'll only hear songs you've never played before. I got one prog rock tip from one of the many iPod-related magazines that began to swamp the market in 2004. This suggested I configure the top row of a pop-up menu to read "Time is greater than 15 minutes." I was told to click the + button and configure the next row to read "Genre is Rock," and then to click the + button once again and configure this row to read "Year is in the Range 1971 to 1979." And to guard against the collection degenerating into a Self-Indulgent Noodling Guitar/Bass/Drum Solo from Hell playlist, I was told to add the following: "Artist is not Grateful Dead."

Tonight my plan is simple: I'm trying to create a playlist of the coolest records ever made. Not the best, but the coolest. Not the ones that make the critics cake the front of their pants, but the ones that look good lying around the house, the ones that look good piled up on the Habitat Daft Punk coffee table or the SCP glass shark . . . the ones to impress your friends with. Personally speaking this is a lot more difficult than it would have been twenty or thirty years ago, when notions of hip were far more prosaic; back then there were only a certain amount of trendy people in the world, but these days everybody's trendy in one way or another, and most people feel confident enough to offer an opinion on the subject. Designer lifestyle culture has grown to such an extent that it has become the predominant culture.

Thirty-odd years ago, back in 1972, when I was eleven, I thought I was the only one who felt different, the only one who was obsessed with pop stars and what they wore, what they said . . . what they didn't say. Sitting in French class, as odd-sounding adverbs swirled around my head, falling on deaf ears, my mind was full of David Bowie's hair, its color, shape, construction. How did he get it that way? What made him think of it? I knew he had this whole space age, glitter thing going on, but honestly, he was so far removed from my life that he may as well have *been* from Mars. Perhaps all would be revealed when I borrowed Bruce's copy of *The Man Who Sold the World* on Friday. What I didn't know was that nearly 5 percent of my generation felt exactly the same way . . . but we were still in the minority.

I've bought some sort of recorded music every week for the past three decades, a thirty-year binge of glam rock, punk rock, disco, and rap. Music has informed every part of my life since before I became a teenager, a life that has included, at various points, the Beatles, David Bowie, the Clash, Chic, Oasis, U2, and ten thousand more.

For three decades my life has been a world full of disparate pop stars and their disparate records. Some have changed the way I think, some have changed the way I act, and some have just been there when I've come home from work in the evening.

In their own way, every record I've bought since the age of eleven has informed my life, however randomly. And then suddenly, when I wasn't looking, Steve Jobs comes along and helps me put it all in one place.

What on Earth was I going to do now?

The iPod has changed my life. The iPod has given me back the ability to obsess over records in the way I did when I was a teenager. But even though my obsession has been rekindled, I consume music in a totally different way than I did five, ten, thirty years ago—we all do. We now consume it laterally, and are just as likely to buy a Bob Dylan compilation or a repackaged Oasis album as we are the new CD from Kelis or Coldplay. We also live in a world that defines itself by anniversaries, and modern pop has to fight for attention/publicity/airplay/marketing budgets with the twenty-fifth-anniversary rerelease of the Clash's *London Calling*, the thirtieth anniversary rerelease of *The Dark Side of the Moon*, and the tenth-anniversary rerelease of Oasis's *(What's the Story) Morning Glory*.

This has all been exacerbated by online music sales and the legalization and legitimization of buying music over the Internet. Instead of taking a lunch break we can now sit behind our desks and download to our laptops to our heart's content. We can click onto iTunes and rip the new Rufus Wainwright album, a sampler from the new R.E.M. CD that you can't buy or hear anywhere else, or a Razorlight tune that has been specially commissioned by Apple and will only be available online. Alternatively you could simply download *Never Mind the Bollocks, Here's the Sex Pistols* and be done with it.

These days, anything goes.

Taste, if we're being honest about it, is determined largely by cost and space. I can't afford a good original Warhol and my house only has enough room for one of those big Conran Shop sofas, the ones that are so huge they make you feel like the Incredible Shrinking Man.

It used to be the same with music.

When I bought the Beatles' double "Blue" album, *1967–1970*, in 1973 (why was I spending over four pounds on a record, my mother demanded to know? What a terrible, unforgivable waste of money—four pounds, on a damn record, your father will be furious!), the first Beatles record I'd ever bought (although I seem to recall my parents had a few singles, "Hey Jude" included), the track listing was the prism through which I appreciated the songs. Was "Ob-La-Di, Ob-La-Da" really the crowning glory of the "White Album"? If I was told it was, then I obviously I believed that. The "Blue" album couldn't possibly house every classic Beatles song, so I got what they could fit onto four sides of vinyl, which was roughly eighty minutes of gear. When the Beatles' *1* appeared thirty years later, the criteria for inclusion was proscriptive, being singles that had actually got to number one (basically every single the band ever released), but with "Blue" it was arbitrary in the extreme.

Which is kind of mad, isn't it? Even when I compiled cassette tapes in my teens, the maximum I could record was two hours (whether I was taping the Top 40 on a Sunday or a friend's James Brown collection), which, when you're talking about the Beatles, barely makes a dent in their oeuvre. I could take the good bits from *Abbey Road* ("You Never Give

Me Your Money," the best Beatles song of them all), all of side two of *A Hard Day's Night*, and the highlights from *Rubber Soul* and *Revolver* (there would have been nothing from *Sgt Pepper's Lonely Hearts Club Band*, which I still think is their worst album by some distance, a sort of psychedelic music-hall knees up), but not much else.

These days everything's available all the time and we're surrounded by the past every minute of every day, hence the preponderance of lists like this.

So what are the coolest records in the world? Most lists of the Greatest Albums Ever Made are, by their very nature, repetitive, and invariably include the same old—and I stress "old"—records. To wit: *Revolver, Astral Weeks, OK Computer, (What's the Story) Morning Glory?, Pet Sounds, Blood on the Tracks, Let It Bleed* (the cake on the cover of which was baked, incidentally, by Delia Smith), *Automatic for the People, Sign o' the Times, Led Zeppelin IV, Dark Side of the Moon, The Queen Is Dead, Achtung Baby, London Calling, Nevermind* . . . the list doesn't so much go on and on as go around in circles.

Whether the lists are compiled by the public or by critics, it's always a case of the usual suspects. These lists are as reliable as Volvos. Occasionally, the odd anomaly will creep in, purely due to current popularity: in one of these lists in *Q* in February 1998, its readers—in their finite wisdom—voted Ocean Colour Scene's *Moseley Shoals* as *the thirty-third greatest album ever made*, which is tantamount to claiming that T. Rex's "I Love to Boogie" is the thirty-third greatest single of all time: objectivity doesn't come into it; it simply isn't true.

Similarly, in 1987, when *Rolling Stone* marshaled together "The 100 Best Albums of the Last 25 Years," in at no.

54—with a bullet!—was Graham Parker's *Howlin' Wind*, a C+ record at the best of times, by a man who sits in the shadow of Bruce Springsteen the way the UK Subs sit in the shadow of the Clash. Bizarre. In the same magazine two years later, in a critics' poll of "The 100 Greatest Albums of the '80s," guess what was ranked no. 19? That's right, Lou Reed's *New York*, not just one of the worst records of his career—one of the worst records of anyone's career. Fifteen or twenty years ago there were still a considerable amount of people—with IQs similar to that of broccoli, obviously—who thought of Lou Reed as a maverick, a cool, urban visionary . . . whereas now we just think of him as, in the words of *GQ* music editor Alexis Petridis, a "grumpy old twat."

These lists emphasize the transient and ephemeral nature of taste, and records that the country held to its collective bosom five years ago can, with the greatest of ease, be cast away like a cardboard coffee cup from Starbucks.

If I want to recall what my life was like before the advent of punk, all I really need to do is look at John Peel's Festive 50 of 1976,[6] which was not only a fair representation of

[6] 1. "Stairway to Heaven" by Led Zeppelin. 2. "Layla" by Derek and the Dominoes. 3. "Desolation Row" by Bob Dylan. 4. "Echoes" by Pink Floyd. 5. "All Along the Watchtower" by Jimi Hendrix. 6. "All Right Now" by Free. 7. "They Shoot Horses Don't They?" by Racing Cars. 8. "Shine on You Crazy Diamond" by Pink Floyd. 9. "A Day in the Life" by the Beatles. 10. "Like a Rolling Stone" by Bob Dylan. 11. "Rose of Cimarron" by Poco. 12. "Cortez the Killer" by Neil Young. 13. "Brown Sugar" by the Rolling Stones. 14. "Hey Jude" by the Beatles. 15. "Paralyzed" by the Legendary Stardust Cowboy. 16. "Voodoo Chile" by Jimi Hendrix. 17. "Strawberry Fields Forever" by the Beatles. 18. "Big Eyed Beans from Venus" by

what his listeners (Me! You!) liked, it was a pretty fair representation of what we all liked. The counterculture was easily defined in those days, even if, at the time, we thought it was nigh invisible to other people. John Peel's death in 2004 affected me in much the same way it affected anyone who had had cause to listen to his Radio 1 program in the past thirty-odd years, causing me to look back at my own life and remember the particular records that had punctuated it. As a Peel listener, one moment sticks in my mind more than any other: I am sitting in my mother's cottage in the wilds of Suffolk in the spring of 1977, having come up to visit for a few days. My parents having separated in 1976, my father

---

Captain Beefheart. 19. "Whole Lotta Love" by Led Zeppelin. 20. "Free Bird" by Lynyrd Skynyrd. 21. "Madame George" by Van Morrison. 22. "Riders on the Storm" by the Doors. 23. "Visions of Johanna" by Bob Dylan. 24. "White Rabbit" by Jefferson Airplane. 25. "Child in Time" by Deep Purple. 26. "Long Distance Love" by Little Feat. 27. "Pickin' the Blues" by Grinderswitch. 28. "Rocky Mountain Way" by Joe Walsh. 29. "Won't Get Fooled Again" by the Who. 30. "I Can Take You to the Sun" by the Misunderstood. 31. "Supper's Ready" by Genesis. 32. "No Woman, No Cry" by Bob Marley and the Wailers. 33. "Roadrunner" by Jonathan Richman. 34. "Maggie May" by Rod Stewart. 35. "Late for the Sky" by Jackson Browne. 36. "Kashmir" by Led Zeppelin. 37. "Hey Joe" by Jimi Hendrix. 38. "Jessica" by the Allman Brothers Band. 39. "Jumping Jack Flash" by the Rolling Stones. 40. "Dark Star" by the Grateful Dead. 41. "I Wanna See the Bright Lights" by Richard Thompson. 42. "The Weaver's Answer" by Family. 43. "Fountain of Sorrow" by Jackson Browne. 44. "Hurricane" by Bob Dylan. 45. "Light My Fire" by the Doors. 46. "O Caroline" by Matching Mole. 47. "When an Old Cricketer Leaves the Crease" by Roy Harper. 48. "Go to Rhino Records" by Wild Man Fischer. 49. "Willin' " by Little Feat. 50. "And You and I" by Yes.

had stayed in High Wycombe while my mother moved back to East Anglia, which is where she pretty much stayed (to be rejoined by my father a few years later). It is around ten-fifteen, and I am listening to the Peel show on giant black headphones, the sort that are so large and so synthetic they leave a cool damp patch covering your ears when you take them off. I am waiting for something in particular, and soon enough it comes, proceeded by Peel simply saying, "Here's Sheena." What follows is one of the greatest intros ever heard on vinyl: "Sheena Is a Punk Rocker," two and a half minutes of Spector-esque power punk, with a hook and a bass line sent straight from God (via Queens, Coney Island, and Rockaway Beach).

The Ramones would eventually recede from my thoughts, although they would reappear, as all records eventually do, in a fashion show—Versace's spring-summer show in July 1999, accompanying Naomi Campbell and a small army of muscle-bound male models as they sashayed down the catwalk, acting out the balletic courtship techniques of streetwise Montagues and Capulets. Since becoming a journalist I have probably been to around two thousand fashion shows (London, Paris, New York, Milan, Barcelona, L.A., Toronto, etc.), and I have to say that the thing that remains with me from a lot of them is the music. The music you hear at fashion shows is never incidental, and can often be the most important aspect of the entire exercise. More than any other social barometer, fashion designers live in the moment, and their choice of music—particularly the way in which it is juxtaposed—can make or break their season. The indiscriminate blips and squeaks that accompany a designer's clothes as models sashay down the catwalk in front of the world's press can be zeitgeist-determining.

It also helps if the designers tap into the correct, fetishistic record of the moment. Each season there will be a song you'll hear two dozen times in the space of six weeks; one season all you heard was "I'm Too Sexy" by Right Said Fred, another season's soundtrack was the first four songs on the Scissor Sisters CD. Fashion show DJs were as important in the development of modern pop as the Bronx house party DJs of the late seventies. Grandmaster Flash and Afrika Bambaataa may have mixed hip-hop beats with the likes of Queen and Kraftwerk, but at the same time, fashion show DJs in Paris and London were mixing Dvořák with Dollar, Pinky and Perky with Irish jigs, heavy metal with Beethoven, and Gregorian chants jumbled up with deafening hi-energy. Models would career down the runway accompanied only by bird noises or the sound of a typewriter, by machine gun fire and orchestral explosions, by Shostakovich and the Sex Pistols. I even tried my hand at it once (albeit unsuccessfully), when I played DJ at the Alternative Fashion Show at St. Martins in 1980, sending Blitz Kids out onstage to the strains of ABBA, Mott the Hoople, George Clinton, and Gary Glitter.

So just what is cool these days? Stuart, my tennis buddy, whom I graciously allow to thrash me every Saturday morning, has a penchant for Chris Rea, a man hitherto unburdened by cool; yet even he (Rea, not Stuart, obviously) has recently been anointed. My brother, Daniel (you may have heard of him; Elton John wrote a song about him), has, for his sins, been the world's number-one ELO fan since God was a boy, and while this may not seem like the coolest thing in the world, is there anyone out there who doesn't harbor a grudging respect for "Mr. Blue Sky" (even though it sounds like "A Day in the Life" as interpreted by Morecambe and Wise)?[7]

What is cool? Well, what was considered hip six months ago is probably a lot different from what was supposed to be hip a year ago, and compared to what was hip five years ago . . . ? Well, you only have to guess. Cool changes with the wind, and often simply because of it. Hip, by its very nature, is fleeting and fickle, and that's as it should be.

There have always been those records that people have always said they liked, always said they listened to in the privacy of their matte-black garrets, but which in all honesty lay untroubled and virginlike in their cardboard sleeves and jewel cases, gathering dust and distain in equal measure. This sort of blind appreciation usually starts with adolescent intellectual one-upmanship, which surely has to be the explanation for the "popularity" of albums such as Jane's Addiction's *Ritual de lo Habitual*, the Blue Nile's *Hats*, and anything by Billy Bragg. The same goes for Patti Smith's *Radio Ethiopia*. I've lost count of the number of flats, houses, and parties I went to in my youth where I saw this lying around nonchalantly, daring someone to play it, having been put there purposefully by some proud but insecure owner. And no one ever played it. Ever. We had all loved *Horses*, and would quite like *Easter* when it came out a year or so later, but *Radio Ethiopia* (a succès d'estime if ever there was one)

[7]My brother is resolute in his convictions, and although it would take some sort of universal seismic volte-face to make Genesis fashionable, he maintains that "Entangled," from *A Trick of the Tail* (their first post–Peter Gabriel LP, from 1976) is his favorite song. Good luck to him, I say.

gave us all a headache. The same goes for Siouxsie and the Banshees' *The Scream*. I liked the idea of Siouxsie a lot, and the pinboard in my room at Ralph West was covered with photographs of her, but while her concerts were amazing, the record stank. When a friend of mine said the only thing Jacques Derrida had in common with Marx was a huge fan club and a great lagoon of unreadness, I knew what he meant.

My subjectivity has produced blind spots too: there are— count them—no songs on my machine by the Doors (I adored them until I spent a year researching and writing a book about them); almost no country (some songs by Lucinda Williams and Johnny Cash, but not much else; country music is often called the music of the Republican Party, whereas I always thought it was music for the after party— i.e., the after-everyone-has-gone-home party); practically no world music (I ran an African club in Soho for a year and that put me off it for life, plus there are only so many times a person can listen to a Gasper Lawal record and that number is zero); no Elvis and only thirty-four reggae songs (I sold most of the stuff I had when I was poor and have never bothered to replace it; well, apart from "Ob-La-Di Ob-La-Da").

Scarcity has proved extremely important when considering what is and what isn't cool, and it's a sad but honest fact that both Neil Young's *On the Beach* and the Beach Boys' *Smile* have both been somewhat diminished by, in the former's case, being released on CD, and in the latter's, being rerecorded, valiantly but in karaoke fashion, by Brian Wilson.

And so here I am, late on a Friday night, lost in thought, lost in music, building the perfect music library, a library that contains every significant piece of music ever recorded, from Strauss and Schubert through Gilbert and Sullivan to

Simon and Garfunkel. As I move through the architecture of iTunes like a digitized motorbike in a computer game, I hit Buddy Holly, the Beatles, the Clash, Dr. Dre, the Monkees, Joy Division, and Franz Ferdinand (the Joy Division Monkees). This box contains all my memories, four decades of the things: friends, lovers, family—they're all in here somewhere. And what is the greatest of them all, the greatest record ever made? With a digital library you are faced with an endless multiplicity of truths, a string of infinite possibilities. Which causes endless, infinite problems: if you've got all this stuff at your fingertips, it makes it very difficult to edit it all down to a small, finite list. In fact the point of the machine is that this small finite list is one of many thousands of such lists, and one way to make sure you have the best is by having everything; then you can't lose.

Capacity is paramount in the world of the Pod. When I decided to get involved, I didn't muck about with any of the smaller capacity machines—15 GB? Are you mad? 20 GB? What do you take me for, eh? No, when I went in, I went in big, and opted for the Big Daddy, the 40 GB. Anything less would have been an embarrassment. Friends of mine have invested in the iPod mini, but even with the silver finish I'm not convinced; after all, when you can squeeze a lifetime into a machine, why settle for just a decade or two?

A few weeks after getting my machine, I began slipping into a predictable pattern of conversation, trying to force everyone I met into having some sort of opinion on this latest technological manifestation of the future. Did they have one, and if not, why not? If they did, what was on it? And why? And after a few polite minutes where I would nod and smile a lot and pretend I was impressed by their esoteric taste ("Oh, you've uploaded all the Police albums, have you? Interesting . . ."), I'd drop the Big Question.

"So, which version do you have? How big is it?"

And if they pretended not to know, or were vague in their response, I'd push some more.

"So, how many songs can you get on it? You know, *how big is it?* Your iPod?"

And then I'd get the downcast eyes, the furrowed brow and the shifting from foot to foot.

"I've, er, got the middle one, you know, the 20."

"The what?" I'd reply, pretending not to have heard? "The 40?"

"No, the 20. The 20 gigabyte. The middle one . . . but I can get loads of songs on it and how many can you really listen to at any one time. I mean, I think it's ridiculous the way people go on about how many songs they can get on their iPod. I mean, it's babyish, isn't it, and anyway I haven't got time to listen to my old records let alone new ones, so actually I'm not sure if it's such a great invention. Anyway, the papers are always full of the things, and I think I'm going to start going back to CDs. I really only got it for my girlfriend and she only likes what's in the charts anyway, so anyway . . ."

So anyway, I would let them blabber on for a while, then mutter "amateur" under my breath and move on to my next victim.

"So, what's on your iPod then?" I'd say, as though I were asking, in a nasally suburban whine, "So, what you driving at the moment then, eh?"

Toward the end of 2004 there developed something of a pissing contest in our office, and water-cooler conversations began to veer away from reality TV, football, the fluctuating fortunes of Sky News, or the latest BlackBerry, to the number of songs on our iPods. And while you may have thought it was perfectly acceptable to casually admit you only have, say, 1,200 songs on your memory box, for a few weeks it was very easy to become an object of derision for not taking this seriously enough. For a while there was definitely a quantity-over-quality issue, a sort of digital penis envy . . .

And although this was a very male thing, I had always thought the iPod was asexual, like a Walkman or a mobile phone. It is, of course, highly sexual, and has an innate, tactile sexuality, but I'd never thought of it as gender specific. It is such a thing of beauty, such an abstract object of desire, yet it is somehow *above all that*. Until I heard someone refer to it as feminine, that is. He—this . . . man!—was describing the JBL On Stage speaker system, a disc-shaped port in which your beloved Pod can nestle, while "unleashing a respectable six watts per channel and charges her up for the day." Her? *Her?* When did the Pod suddenly become feminine? How did that happen? Was I away that day, toying with Microsoft or Sony? I think it was fairly obvious that the iPod minis, in all their metallic (adonized aluminium) pastel glory, were aimed at the female market, but was this chap really saying my chrome 40 GB 3G monster wasn't masculine, that he was somehow "not as other hardware"?

And so overnight my iPod became male, just because someone had said it was feminine. Pathetic of me, I know. But very male all the same. And if the iPod is gender specific, then my machine is an Ivan rather than an Irene (hairless though it may be). And anyway, in France it's *le iPod*, not *la*. So there.

Jonathan Ive, who is an industrial designer first and a soothsayer second, is adamant that it's neither. An unaffected man, he says that in his eyes the iPod isn't sexual at

all. "The iPod is not masculine or feminine, and if the appeal
was just about the look, then it wouldn't be compelling for
very long. It's a small, white, plastic and chrome music
player. The object was always to make the nicest music
player possible." (My friend Stuart, who is a diplomat by
profession as well as at play, complicated matters by calling
it "metrosexual," which I didn't think was helpful at all.)

Yet anthropomorphizing my iPod wasn't going to help it
orchestrate a list of the coolest records in the world. I'd have
to do that.

But as soon as I start I get sidetracked. As I begin poring
over my Steely Dan playlist (which contains everything they'd
ever released, including "Dallas" and "Sail the Waterway"
from a mid-seventies EP, as well as a bootleg copy of "The
Second Arrangement," the great lost song from *Gaucho*), I
start doing due diligence on *Aja*, trying to work exactly why
it's the best record ever made (not the coolest, you understand, just the best). I feel like one of those early computer
programmers, those educated young men of disheveled appearance, with glowering sunken eyes and megalomaniacal
fantasies of omnipotence.

Then I wander off into the Beach Boys, then Van Morrison, then Coldplay . . . oh, it is becoming oh so predictable
and oh so boring. And so I think back to when I was seventeen, when being "cool" probably occupied my thoughts
more than at any time before or after, and wonder what I'd
feel like if I were like that today, and every consumer decision was based on how other people would interpret it.
What (twenty, say) records would I leave lying around the
house? What albums would I have sitting in the car? What
would I keep open on my iTunes in case anyone wandered
past my PowerBook?

Well, right now, as I'm writing this, they are as follows, in no particular order:

(1) *Back in the USA* by the MC5 (a classic proto-punk record that still sounds like it can't believe it's so excited)

(2) *Sign o' the Times* by Prince (a veritable smorgasbord, and the best album of the eighties)

(3) *Kind of Blue* by Miles Davis (a record impervious to criticism or fashion)

(4) *London Calling* by the Clash (ditto)

(5) *Isaac Hayes Live at the Sahara Tahoe* (the best soul album ever recorded)

(6) *The College Dropout* by Kanye West (2004's nomination for the best hip-hop album ever made)

(7) Any obscure Johnny Cash album (the worse the better)

(8) *Grace* by Jeff Buckley (a hardy perennial)

(9) *Two Sevens Clash* by Culture (the best punk reggae album)

(10) *Solid Air* by John Martyn (*One World* is better but this is cooler)

(11) Any Kraftwerk album (literally any; they all do what they're supposed to)

(12) *The Koln Concert* by Keith Jarrett (the best piano album ever made)

(13) *Waltz for Koop* by Koop (good, but obscure—so great)

(14) *Physical Graffiti* by Led Zeppelin (once banished, they're now back forever)

(15) *The Bends* by Radiohead (works in every country in the world)

(16) *Everest* by the Beatles (it doesn't exist, so you'll have to make it up)

(17) *The Libertines* by the Libertines (it's better than their first record and don't let anyone tell you otherwise)

(18) *World Without Tears* by Lucinda Williams (a sexy Tom Waits)

(19) *The Crickets* by Marcos Valle (you'll never find it)

(20) *Aftermath* by the Rolling Stones (the epitome of Swinging London).

But I realize I've forgotten to include *Goodbye Yellow Brick Road* (Elton's coolest record, even though it doesn't include "Tiny Dancer"; he was originally going to call it *Vodka and Tonic*), *Elephant Mountain* by the Youngbloods ("Sunrise" is officially a better ballad than "Yesterday"), *Dusty in Memphis*, and a thousand more . . .

12

How "i" Learned to Stop Worrying and Love Jazz

It's big, it's clever, it's grown-up

So there I was, in the large HMV near Selfridges on London's Oxford Street, some time in April, around four-thirty on a Friday afternoon. I'd just dropped about eighty pounds—on *Elephant* by the White Stripes, Blur's *Think Tank*, a second copy of the Strokes' first album, a new Marmalade compilation (their "I See the Rain" has recently been used in a Gap ad), plus *The Last Waltz* and *The Wicker Man* on DVD. On top of all this I had, uncharacteristically, also spent another forty pounds on three jazz CDs: one fairly useless acid jazz compilation and two of the greatest records I'd heard in over a year, John Coltrane's *Giant Steps* and Duke Ellington's *Far East Suite*. I bought them on a whim, at the suggestion of friends, two suggestions that have changed my life in considerable ways.

Every week since then I've been going back for more, building up a jazz library that threatens to dwarf everything else in my collection. Having kept jazz pretty much at arm's length for the best part of my life, I've found myself embracing it as an estranged father might embrace his long-lost kin. Getting into jazz is like suddenly discovering you have an extended family you knew nothing about, although the family in question runs to thousands of members. Like turning the world upside down and finding another one underneath, a world where they only ever listen to jazz.

I even have a playlist—of course I have a playlist!—devoted to jazz. I haven't called it anything cute yet; it's just called jazz, rather weedily (no inverted commas, nothing), as though I couldn't really be bothered to call it anything else, as though I'm somehow embarrassed about it, but I'm not. It's probably just because it's a work in progress, which it most obviously is. With every other playlist I think I'm pretty much there, you know what I mean? Of course I'm going to add the next Coldplay album in its entirety—and probably the one after that and the one after that—and I occasionally get converted to things I used to hate (Jeff Buckley, Led Zeppelin, ELO—I now have more ELO in iTunes than I do Oasis). But I don't feel I have to wade through all of Jimi Hendrix's back catalog—I've done that, thanks, and don't much care for it. Is there much rock music I didn't really know I liked? Are there many Spooky Tooth or Fairport Convention albums out there I don't know about but will fall in love with at some point over the next ten years? Maybe, maybe even probably, but I've spent thirty years covering the waterfront, so I think I know what I'm talking about (Van Morrison and Nick Drake are good; Simple Minds and the Doors are crap—you get the gist). But with jazz, I'm still pretty much at a loss. My current playlist has 653 songs on it, enough for a good holiday weekend—2.1 days, 3.67 GB. There's a lot of Miles Davis, a lot of classic

Blue Note, and tons of bossa nova, but nothing too difficult. I don't like difficult jazz; I find it too . . . well, difficult. And annoying and self-serving and unnecessarily complicated and pretentious and unwieldy . . . but mostly just difficult.

My newfound fascination started during a boys' trip to Japan, for the World Cup in 2002. Oliver, Andrew, and I (Peyton, Hale, & Jones, solicitors to the glitterati) had all got permission slips from our wives to go to Japan for the two weeks of group games, where we would watch the three England and three Ireland games. I'd been to Japan twice before and had always been blown away by the place—technologically, architecturally, culturally . . . Ironically—really ironically—one of the country's most significant cultural characteristics was its carpetbagging of Western pop culture, which it ate up with Pac-Man-like zeal. The Japanese were very good at appropriating the methods and styles of fashion and pop without ever having to experience the catharsis of original birth, that is. When I first went, in 1983 (to model in a fashion show for the Men's Bigi label, of all things, having been approached by some scouts in a Soho nightclub called, rather appropriately, White Trash), the record shops were full of knockoff pop, and you could tell what the albums sounded like just be looking at the covers. When I went again in 1996, to catalog Paul Smith's ascendancy as Britain's greatest cultural export (at every public appearance he was mobbed like no Brit had been mobbed since the Beatles thirty years previously), the music had improved considerably, although it was still derivative. But when I walked into the Beams record store in Shinjuku-ku in Tokyo in May 2002 (a sort of shining twenty-first-century Xanadu of pop), I was presented with thousands of cool-looking CDs, none of which had covers that gave any indication as to what they contained. In between the low garble of generic U.S. hip-hop and weirder-than-weird Japanese pop, the in-house stereo began pumping out this mad, disjointed, almost insane jazz arrangement. The assistant told me it was *Electric Bath* by the Don Ellis Orchestra, and it was simply the maddest thing I'd ever heard, and the sort of thing you tend to only hear in Tokyo record shops. So I bought it and vowed to properly delve into the jazz labyrinth as soon as I got back to London.

When I told my friends about my new quest, Andrew was both indulgent and helpful, suggesting dozens of records, including a whole bunch of rare Herbie Hancock LPs. Oliver, meanwhile, was typically dismissive: "Jazz? What do you want to listen to that for? It's all fuckin' shite" (which, to be honest, is what Oliver tends to say about everything unless he discovers it first).

While I was compiling my playlist, jazz started to replace every other form of music in my life. If I were on *Desert Island Discs*, I thought to myself rather conceitedly at one point, what would I bring? Would any of them be jazz records? What about if I brought only jazz records? After all, what would be the point of bringing your eight favorite records with you? Wouldn't it be better to take eight things you didn't know, eight records you could grow to love just by dint of listening to them ad infinitum? What would be the point of taking your favorite Aphex Twin, U2, and Earth Wind & Fire records if you're going to hear them day in, day out for the rest of your life? It's something of a pointless exercise, I know, but how many times can you listen to the first side of *Moondance* before it begins to pall? Why not just take a shitload of jazz, eight of the maddest, longest, most out-there jazz records in the shop? But then I remembered I didn't like the difficult stuff and calmed down a bit.

After my expressway-to-Damascus experience, I became a man possessed. Only five minutes after meeting someone I would ask them what their favorite jazz record was. Experts were eager to please, friends couldn't stop suggesting things. One introduced me to lots of (very good) jazz guitarists, not knowing that I have a natural aversion to anyone sporting a mullet; so that ruled our Pat Metheny, Mike Stern, Frank Gambale, and a lot of decidedly odd Germans. I also developed an aversion to "soft jazz," and foreswore the likes of Spyro Gyra, David Sanborn, and the kind of soporific stuff I always seem to hear whenever I accidentally turn on Jazz FM.

Not a week went by without me adding to my iTunes library. In my obsession I even resorted to buying some of those "100 Greatest Jazz Hits" CD compilations you find in petrol stations, the kind compiled by people who think Al Jarreau and Glenn Miller are cut from the same cloth (people who might even think that Al Jarreau and Glenn Miller are the same person).

I began compiling an imaginary list of the best jazz records of all time, a list that started to occupy my every waking thought. I'd be in a meeting at work, trying to figure out a way to squeeze a piece about the Angolan civil war into six pages (difficult, but not impossible), and I'd begin comparing the respective voices of Sarah Vaughan and Ella Fitzgerald (was "Lullaby of Birdland" better than "Ev'ry Time We Say Goodbye"? Who knew?). I'd be halfway through a client pitch and begin wondering if Dexter Gordon's "Getting Around" was more impressive than his "Our Man in Paris" (I'm still undecided on this one). If you've ever made lists of your favorite rock songs about California, your favorite punk singles, disco twelve-inches, songs with the name of your girlfriend or wife in them; if you read *High Fidelity* and immediately rushed off to make your own list of Top Ten Breakup Records; if you're still reluctant to give up the clandestine obsessions of your youth, by which I mean being unable to stop yourself from trawling through record-shop racks mentally totting up the CDs you already have . . . if you've ever done any of these things, then you'll know what I'm talking about.

So how do you build a collection? How do you compile the perfect jazz iPod playlist? (Could you fill up an iPod with just jazz?) What do you do once you've summoned up the courage to wander off into the jazz section, what do you buy? Not only is there just so much . . . *stuff*, but there's more stuff every day. It's an ever-expanding world, the jazz world. I mean, even if you knew everything there was to know about jazz, how could you possibly own it all? There are nearly as many jazz albums as there are women in the world, and how could you sleep with all of *them*? As with any other type of music, there are some classic records you'd be mad to ignore, but with jazz you really have to plough your own furrow. The jazz police are a proscriptive lot— look to them for recommendations and they'll tell you that Norah Jones and Stan Getz aren't jazz, that Blue Note shouldn't have signed St. Germain, and that Dave Brubeck's "Take Five" is only ever good for paint commercials. However, these are probably the same people who, twenty-five years ago, would have told you that ABBA don't make good pop music, or that punk was a flash in the pan.

But there were certainly things I just didn't get. Ornette Coleman was one of them. At the same time as Miles Davis was breaking through with modal jazz forms, Ornette Coleman invented free jazz with *The Shape of Jazz to Come*. Nearly fifty years after the event it is difficult to recapture the shock that greeted the arrival of this record, but *Shape* just gave me a headache. Coleman played a white plastic saxophone that looked like a toy and was a master of the one-liner, the "Zen zinger" (stuff like, "When the band is playing with the drummer, it's rock 'n' roll, but when the drummer is playing with the band, it's jazz"), so I really, really wanted to like his music. But I couldn't, no matter how much I tried. As far as I was concerned, he was improvising up his own sphincter.

And what is jazz anyway? Is it Koop's *Waltz for Koop,* a Swedish approximation of loungecore jazz, or is it Terry Callier's *Turn You to Love,* which is almost deep soul but is released on Elektra's "classic jazz" label. The truth is, jazz is a bit of everything, something that isn't so surprising when you consider it was born out of marching band, the blues, minstrel music, and New Orleans creole. Jazz is Dixieland, swing, fusion, jazz-funk, jazz-rock, R&B, bossa nova, be-bop, hard bop, hip-hop, cool jazz, hot jazz, West Coast jazz, modal jazz, acid jazz, soul jazz, free jazz, trad jazz, modern cheroot-smoking Sta-Prest button-down jazz, the lot. Some people now even call it the new chill-out (fools). Let's hope not. Chill-out has always seemed, to my jaundiced ears at least, a rather pejorative term, implying a type of music you listen to *(a)* when coming down from drugs, or *(b)* the morning/afternoon after a heavy drug binge, when all your fragile temperament can cope with is some feint break beats, some aimless keyboard doodling, and rudimentary A-level acoustic guitar. For chill-out read *drop out*.

Not everyone I ask about jazz is as enthusiastic as I am.

There are some people who will never like it; as the *Daily Telegraph's* Martin Gayford wrote recently: "You can tell there must be something good about modern art just by considering the people who hate it—and the same is true of jazz." Jazz is for people who don't like music, says my friend Bill; it must be fun to play, he says, because it sure ain't fun to listen to ("I remember this tune," he'll say, warming to his theme, "which is more than I can say for the guy playing it"). It is, in the words of some forgotten 1980s comedian, six guys onstage playing different tunes. *GQ* ran a joke about it a while back: Q: "Why do some people instantly hate jazz?" A: "It saves time in the long run." Even my six-year-old daughter hates it. After being subjected to hours of Charlie Parker in the car one weekend, she said, as though I hadn't realized it myself, "I don't like this music. There are no songs for me to sing to." (The only jazz tune she likes is "Everybody Wants to Be a Cat," from Disney's *The Aristocats*, which, actually, has a great sound track—honestly.[8]) Unbeknownst to her, she was echoing John Lennon's little-known jibe: "Jazz never does anything."

Some people's innate hatred of jazz is simply the result of an unfortunate experience, but then anyone who's witnessed Art Blakey performing a three-and-a-half-hour drum solo is entitled to feel a little peeved (and I speak as someone who has seen one at close quarters, at Ronnie Scott's back in the mid-1980s, when, for about three months, jazz was unfeasi-

---

[8]Musically I have tried to indoctrinate both my daughters, but with limited success, and while I've succeeded with the Beatles (Georgia likes "the Octopus song") and the Strokes, many musical milestones have turned into millstones. Particular favorites remain the Monkees, Justin Timberlake, Kylie Minogue, and the Scissor Sisters.

bly trendy). On top of this, some people just don't get it. Like the later work of James Joyce and the films of Tarkovsky, the fact that some things will always live just beyond the common understanding is something jazz enthusiasts must learn to live with. Heigh-ho.

Also, jazz has often been victim to the vagaries of fashion, destined to be revived at the most inappropriate moments. The last time jazz was really in the limelight was, as I said, back in the mid-1980s, when it became the soundtrack du jour in thousands of matt-black bachelor flats all over designer Britain, and when every style magazine and beer ad seemed to look like a Blue Note album cover. Jazz went from being a visceral, corporeal music to a lifestyle soundtrack. This was the age of the Style Council, of *Absolute Beginners* . . . of Sting. Buying into jazz was meant to lend your life a patina of exotic sophistication, and was used to sell everything from Filofaxes and coffee machines to designer jeans and sports cars.

In his excellent book *Jazz 101: A Complete Guide to Learning and Loving Jazz*, John F. Szwed wrote: "The life and look of the black jazz musician offered a double attraction, that of the alienations of both artist and colour. Whatever jazz might have been as an actual occupation, the jazz musician offered one of the first truly nonmechanical metaphors of the 20th Century. Now, whether one has heard of Charlie Parker of not, we inherit a notion of cool, an idea of well-etched individuality, a certain angle of descent." If jazz had started life as a subversive sexual extension of ragtime, blues, boogie-woogie, and the New Orleans sound, by the end of the century it had become the soundtrack of accomplishment, a way of upstairs acknowledging downstairs in the manner of nostalgie de la boue.

But what about the music? In many ways, and for many people, jazz ended in the early 1960s, when Ornette Coleman, John Coltrane, and Cecil Taylor suddenly became the avant-garde; in fact, almost everything that has happened to jazz in the last forty years could be called "post-Coltrane" in much the same way that people use "postmodern." Obviously jazz didn't end then, but its public persona did; either jazz was "free" and difficult (mad-looking Belgians with crazy hair, billowing luminescent smocks, and angular clarinet-looking instruments), or else it was nostalgic (Harry Connick Jr. et al). Ironically, for a type of music so obsessed with the modern and the "now," jazz has always been preoccupied with the past, so much so that during the 1980s and 1990s it became less and less able to reflect modern culture. Everyone wanted to sound like Miles or Dizzy; either that, or they went fusion mad and ended up sounding and looking like Frank Zappa on steroids.

And so, after six long months, I arrived at my final selection, the hundred best jazz CDs money can buy, the CDs that would produce the playlist on my iPod. The selections aren't necessarily all benchmarks; they're simply the best records to listen to, the ones that give me the most pleasure. For a while it seemed like my mission was simply to collect as many versions of "A Night in Tunisia" as I could (and I did—my library now contains three killer versions, by Charlie Parker, Dexter Gordon, and Dizzy Gillespie, as well as a vocal version by Eddie Jefferson that I'm still not sure about), although I eventually branched out into all areas of jazz, from New York stride piano to the Third Stream stuff (the classical-jazz crossover). There is very little trad, not much fusion, and rather a lot of stuff from the golden age of modern jazz, from 1955 to 1965. Oh, and nine albums by Miles Davis (eight of which have been uploaded in their entirety).

Three years ago I could never have pictured myself wearing a metaphorical beret and nodding along to seemingly random trumpet sounds in the comfort of my own home. But here I am, imagining myself looking out over Los Angeles from Case Study House No. 22, with an AVO Classic Robusto in one hand and a large glass of amarone in the other. And all I can hear is Freddie Hubbard. Mmmm, jazz. *Nice.*

13.

iPod, uPod, We All Shop for iPod

In New York, the birth of a retail revolution

New York: The Sunday afternoon sun is dipping behind the extravagantly upholstered lofts and warehouses of SoHo. Along Prince Street, hordes of itinerant shoppers slope from vaulted window to vaulted window. They graze through the stores, their outsize cardboard carrier bags banging against their legs as they go. In New York, shopping in the "Naughties" is still devotional, and although they give the impression of being collectively absentminded, the hundreds of baseball-capped, Gap-legged, and Nike-topped New Yorkers strolling along Prince Street and Broadway this autumn afternoon have a purposeful glint in their eyes.

Nowhere is this glint more discernible than in Station A, on the corner of Prince and Green, just along from the gargantuan Prada store, and just around the corner from the hideously fashionable Mercer Hotel, where the media meet for latte and gossip. Here, a mass of excitable yet slow-footed consumers look as though they have died and gone to shopping heaven. As computer technology has become the new religion, so Apple's Station A is its shrine.

Here is a world that offers so much in the shape of so much color and speed, so many permutations of brushed metal and neoprene, and as many sorts of software as there are gigabytes on your average hard disc. There are currently seventy Apple stores in the United States, and though satellite operations are opening up all over the world—each one with the same manufactured feeling of austere indulgence, each one decorated with Apple's trademark blueberry, graphite, and lime—the New York store is the mothership, the lode star, the Starship Enterprise of Apple's brave new world. In a comprehensive and rather remarkable way, Apple has imbued consumerism with a new kind of dignity.

Since it opened at the turn of the century, Station A has become something of a mecca, and has attracted the kind of adulatory talk usually reserved for monolithic clothing stores (Barney's, Comme Des Garçons, Prada). New York does gentrification well—especially in this part of town—but the Apple store has become something else again: it looks like some sort of postmodern church, a digital dreamland. With cash registers. It is the apple of the Big Apple's eye.

This is why Station A is so popular with the trend-weary deities of downtown Manhattan. There is iCandy everywhere. Here, laptops and digital music players are presented as choice exhibits in a traveling exhibition, on podiums and in glass boxes, demanding attention; mouse mats and Fire-Wire adaptors have a reverential air about them; neckband headphones and HotWire cables are displayed as though they are valuable works of art (which to Apple they sort of are; this is an expensive world with copper-bottom built-in margins: an iPod-friendly armband, which is made merely of rubber and a small amount of plastic, can be yours for $30, and the store also offers iPod engraving, for $19.99).

Apple instills its products with a kind of holy superiority, implying entry to this virtuous and meritorious world can be sanctioned simply by investing in an iBook or a PowerPod Auto Adaptor (they even sanctify third-party products). When you slip in a pair of iPod earbuds connected to a brand-spanking-new fourth-generation memory box, and you spin the click-wheel onto a brand-new download by Tom Baxter or an archive classic from Van Dyke Parks (I would suggest "Another Dream" from *Clang of the Yankee Reaper*), then you know that with just one single purchase you could become one of the chosen, one of the new-style great and the good, a member of Apple's seemingly inexhaustible army of consumers.

And boy do they consume: they buy iMacs, PowerBooks, iPods ("I still think it looks like a bar of soap, Martha"), iTrips, miniature Altec Lansing speakers so they can listen to their iPod in their kitchens and their hotel rooms, Bluetooth wireless headphones, Tivoli radios, Lilipod waterproof iPod cases (or "skins" as they're known), Xtreme iPod car chargers, every third-party accessory you can imagine. The iPod is now an industry, one that will soon be bigger than the music industry itself.

But how many iPods can Apple really sell? There are only so many pairs of ears in the world, only so many people prepared to succumb to the latest marketing wizardry of a company like this.

Many of the people in Station A are the same people I saw at the Franz Ferdinand concert at Roseland last night, a random army of chino- and backpack-clad endomorphs, keen-eyed yet disorientated, as though they've just walked mistakenly into a recently finished space-age theme park . . . looking for ways to either enter the future or reacquaint themselves with their past (wondering if they can squeeze their own fantasy singles collection into the same sonic universe, or simply pondering the possibility of trying to like Maroon 5—it can be done) . . . wandering around, lost in their own little iWorlds. Many of the semi-shaven East Village–type boys wear wraparound reflective sunglasses and three-quarter-legged trousers while the girls wear short denim skirts, crop-tops, and white Birkenstocks. Apple hasn't just made it easy for its customers to take its products out of the study and into the living room—they can take them anywhere they like, to the banks of the Ganges or the streets of Manhattan.

A lot of the pilgrims here today are regulars, and you can tell they know the store as well as they know their own apartments (and seeing that New York apartments are so small, they might know it a bit better). I bump into two labelholics from London, one of whom has his iPod tucked tightly inside his black patent leather Helmut Lang iPod case, bought at great cost from Colette, the insufferably trendy shop near Place Vendôme in Paris. He couldn't be more pleased when I notice it.

It's a fact that Apple has produced a generation of Mac users who spend half their time gushing effusively about all things Apple (iMacs, iPods, iPhoto, iMovie, iTunes, etc.) and half their time bitching about the performance of all things Apple (they also bitch about the company's seemingly dismissive attitude toward its customer, its secretive, paranoid attitude toward the press, its obsession with discontinuing product lines, its general intransigence . . .). Every Apple product has a forum, a user group, and several dozen Web sites (sometimes several hundred Web sites) devoted to it, where fans and fanatics can obsess to their hearts' content.

Every new ergonomic slab of silicon and polycarbonate is dissected with boffinlike precision, and Apple's True Believers are fiercely protective of their toys: if they feel the company has let them down, they tell it so (in no uncertain terms). Again and again and again.

Take thirty-four-year-old David Glickman, a management consultant from San Francisco. Since buying his iPod in 2003, he has since invested in the following PodAccessories: a pair of noise-canceling headphones, some Sony minispeakers, an FM radio transmitter, various adapters for charging his iPod in his car, a state-of-the-art cable to connect his toy to his stereo, and an adaptor so he and a family member can listen to his tunes simultaneously.

But Mac users' shopping habits caused Apple's commercial rebirth. Big time. In October 2004 Apple announced its fiscal fourth-quarter earnings had more than doubled. It was the company's highest fourth-quarter revenue in nine years, with a net profit of $106 milllion, or 26 cents per share, for the quarter ending September 25. That compared with a profit of $44 million, or 12 cents per share, in the same period in 2003. Sales were $2.35 billion, up 37 percent from $1.72 billion the previous year. "We shipped over two million iPods, our retail store revenues grew 95 percent year over year, and the new iMac G5 has received phenomenal reviews and is off to a great start," said Steve Jobs, rather too matter-of-factly. These two million sales represented a 500 percent increase from the same period the year before, while in the previous quarter Apple had sold 860,000 iPods. Sales of Macintosh computers reached 836,000, a 6 percent increase from 2003's final quarter. As soon as Jobs made the announcement, shares surged by 6 percent, leveling off at $42.15, more than double the level from the year before. In the space of two years Apple had gone from being a $6-billion-a-year company to a $12-billion-a-year company, while the iPod itself had become a $2-billion-a-year business. The third-party businesses were booming too, with both Altec Lansing and Griffin Technology seeing huge, huge rises in profits.

Jobs believes that we are still in the foothills of the digital music revolution. iTunes, the store, has now sold more than 150 million songs worldwide, but although they own 70 percent of the global market (their closest rival, Napster, has 11 percent), this is still a tiny fraction of total music sales. Pascal Cagni, Apple's European boss, says, "The iTunes music store is the key driver to establish the iPod as the Walkman of the twenty-first century."

It's a comparison that preys on Jobs's mind. Since the Walkman was introduced in 1979, Sony has sold over three hundred million of them; so far, Apple has sold a mere six million iPods, more than half of them in the last twelve months. Not only do they have to build on this success, but they have to hold on to their dominance in the market. Critics, including Microsoft's Bill Gates, have repeatedly suggested that Apple is in danger of repeating its mistake with the Macintosh in the eighties, by pinning its faith exclusively on its own technology—this time on the AAC music file format as opposed to the MP3 format that everyone else uses (and that includes Microsoft). But Jobs is nothing if not bullish: Hewlett-Packard now sells its own PC-friendly version of the iPod (nicknamed the hPod), considerably increasing Apple's distribution power, while Jobs's deal with Motorola (enabling users to transfer music from iTunes directly to handheld technology) means Apple will be able to tap into the five-hundred-million-plus handset market with a proven technology and brand, in the hopes of having attach rates in the tens of millions, as opposed to the few million iPods it has currently shipped, and thus dramatically expand the iTunes user base (the future doesn't just mean iTunes direct to your mobile; it means digital entertainment direct to your TV monitor, your hob, your sunglasses, anything you damn well like; LG Electronics have already produced one such gimmick, the Internet Fridge, a £6,000 beast that has already found a home with those paragons of conspicuous consumption, the Beckhams).

The Hewlett-Packard deal was a big one, and analysts predict that HP's hPod will eventually outsell Apple's iPod, given HP's enormous distribution channels. Jobs's decision to open up iTunes and iPod to Windows users was widely praised; one analyst, Charles Wolf from Needham & Co., welcomed it, saying, "In our opinion, Apple's decision to port iTunes to the Windows platform was the most strategically significant one the company made since Steve Jobs' return in 1997. It signalled that Apple would no longer confine its award-winning software to the Mac, but instead leverage it to address a market where 95 percent of consumers use Windows PCs."

The HP product bought into the Apple cult by launching durable, water-resistant Printable Tattoos, special iSkins that could be wrapped around the hPods. They allowed customers to personalize the look of their memory boxes with album cover art, as well as create their own designs and photos to print on Tattoo media via HP color printers. And who wouldn't want to buy into that?

When Apple and Hewlett-Packard announced the deal, then–HP CEO Cary Fiorina said, "We explored a range of alternatives to deliver a great digital-music experience and concluded Apple's iPod music player and iTunes music service were the best by far. We have the opportunity to add value by integrating the world's best digital-music offering into HP's larger digital-entertainment-system strategy."

Apple recognizes that the iPod is a better-known product than the Macintosh, which until recently was its hero product. When it started advertising the Mac G5 in the summer of 2004, the advertising tagline proclaimed the product was "From the creators of iPod," which was tantamount to saying the iPod was Apple's Trojan horse. The new-look Mac showed how serious Apple was about selling computers, and by associating the G5 with the music carrier basically said that if you bought an iPod, then what you really needed was a cool new Mac to go with it.

This had been happening ever since Apple launched the iPod, back in the autumn of 2001, and while its share of the personal computer market was small—it has hovered around 3 percent for years—people began swapping their PCs for Macs because of iPod compatibility (no matter that they could actually use their iPods with their PC if they had the right adapter).

What defines a decade is obviously not a technological invention, but rather a shift in price and performance that triggers a rush from lab to marketplace. Along with Microsoft, Apple has largely been responsible for orchestrating that shift. For a while we weren't sure why any of us out here in the real world needed computers—they did stuff, really quite clever stuff, but why would a person need such a thing? Why would we want a glorified abacus? Using a computer back in the eighties was a consumer decision, not any sort of necessity. In 1943, when the founder of IBM, Thomas Watson, was asked how he viewed the future of technology, his response, it is said, was that there would one day be a world-wide market "for maybe five computers." Soon we won't be able to live our lives without them whether we like it or not.

The year 2004 wasn't all good for Apple though. In July Steve Jobs underwent life-saving pancreatic cancer surgery, and on his return to work the company was once again embroiled in the Apple Computer–versus–Apple Corp. lawsuit that for months had been talked about as potentially the largest non–class action settlement in history. Following the health scare, Jobs sent a memo to his staff, telling them his cancer was a far more curable form of pancreatic cancer than most. Ever the company man, he finished the missive by writing: "I'm sending this from my hospital bed using my 17-inch PowerBook and an Airport Express."

Then there was the furor over the amount Apple was charging U.K. iTunes customers for downloads—79 pence, which at the time was approximately 1.15 euros. Apple's French and German customers at the time were being charged just 0.99 euros—about 67.8 pence. This was contravening European law, which explicitly states that U.K. consumers are supposed to enjoy the same benefits of the single market as other citizens of E.U. member states.

However the future is bright—the future is Apple green. Given that the company's global market share is only about 3 percent industry analysts believe that it will increase substantially since its "mind share" of the PC market seems much higher now that the iPod has revitalized the brand and its product line is refreshed.

As I climb the stairs to Station A's mezzanine, on my way to the book department, I inadvertently walk into the middle of a seminar on iTunes. Some good-meaning soul—who, I soon discover, knows more about selling soap than he does about the internal workings of the iPod—is addressing about fifty wide-eyed innocents, steering them haphazardly through the labyrinthine wonders of all things Mac. He is rushing as he is running out of time, yet is still encouraging his slack-jawed audience to ask him questions. And so I do. But having failed to answer three questions successfully (I'm especially interested in changing encoders and the optimum bit rate of AAC conversion), he spends the rest of the session ignoring my raised hand.

I feel kind of vindicated, in a silly, babyish sort of way. Meet Dylan Jones, I think to myself: iExpert, iBore.

14.

Ask Not What You Can Do For Your iPod, Ask What Your iPod Can Do For You

"I Want My MP3"

It's August 2004 and I am having breakfast at 7, a café in Playa d'en Bossa, where the Manumission podium dancers traditionally come after finishing their eight-hour stint and before they traipse off to the after-party at Space, a few hundred yards away (not for recreation either; there they'll dance some more). They come for beers, café con leche, ensamadas (Spanish croissants, basically, with the consistency of compressed doughnuts), and to soak their feet in plastic washing-up bowls full of warm soapy water.

There are five of them, and seven of us; they've been up for twenty-four hours while we've only been up for two. They're still dripping with sweat; we're just covered in recently applied Auto-Bronzant, the sort that gives you an automatic tan while you're waiting for a real one. Nevertheless we're all enjoying the same soundtrack, the same filtered noise oozing quietly from the café's overhead speakers. It's about nine-thirty and the Tuesday morning sun is already high above the crenelated adobes on this side of the island. There are people everywhere—some dressed in the regulation Day-Glo, logo-intensive sportswear worn by serious clubbers, some simply in tie-dye three-quarter-length shorts and loose-fitting surfer singlets. Unlike at other resorts, unlike at other beaches, in fact, unlike anywhere else in the world, you can't tell whether these people have been up for hours or days. Take a closer peek and some of them look like they've been up for years.

We sit there in all our finery, faces tilted to the sun, nodding along to the music, the girls all in flowing shimmery things, and the boys dressed in the modern Balearic summer wardrobe: Birkenstocks, loud shorts, even louder shirts, and expensive reflective and very girly sunglasses. This is the Ibiza look: young, glitzy, a little too flashy. Men on holiday tend to dress at least five years younger than they normally do, which allows us to indulge ourselves with stuff we wouldn't dream of entertaining at home.

The in-house music at 7 is as eclectic as music is everywhere on this island, as eclectic as it's been for thirty years, as it was thirty years ago, back in the days when Ibiza first started making a name for itself as the alternative egalitarian party capital of the world. Thirty years ago, if you had been sitting here—right where I am now, watching a bunch of podium dancers wash their feet in the hot morning sun—or hereabouts, you would have heard anything from James Brown ("Give It Up or Turn It a Loose") and George McCrae ("Rock Your Baby") to Pink Floyd ("Money") and Roy Harper ("One of Those Days in England"). Today is no different, in essence, only more so. The only difference is, it's not just in Ibiza this is happening; it's happening everywhere, all over the world, in nightclubs and in cafés and bed-rooms from New Cross to New Delhi.

As we sit and sip our coffee, the stereo—such an old-fashioned word these days—pumps out a selection of tunes that encapsulates the way we all consume pop nowadays: the Rolling Stones' "19th Nervous Breakdown" is followed by the handbag house remix of Lou Reed's "Satellite of Love," which in turn is followed by John Barry's lounge-core classic theme from *The Persuaders*, the 2002 bootleg remix of the Velvet Underground's "I'm Waiting for My Man," and at least three club records of unfamiliar prove-nance (at least to me). It wasn't so long ago that having eclectic musical taste was anathema to the average punter. Ever since the dawn of pop—fifty years ago, when Elvis proved that white men really could sing the blues—youth culture has been defined by musical attrition, not musical détente. You liked rockabilly or you liked Motown; you liked Captain Beefheart or you liked the Skatalites; you liked Genesis or the Clash; Womack and Womack or the Je-sus and Mary Chain. You never liked both, and if you did, you weren't really taken seriously.

It is in Ibiza where I have my iPod crisis of confidence. We are on holiday in this huge, mad house, the sort of place the Addams Family might have stayed had they been part of the ecstasy generation. It is a Gothic monument to kitsch com-plete with a forty-eight-track recording studio, a DVD porn den, a snooker room, lap pools, a walk-in wardrobe full of what I assume are lap dancers' wigs, a wigwam (obviously), two miniature ponds, and a fantastically bad sculpture gar-den. When we describe the place to potential visitors, we say it is heartening to know that it is still possible to spend a mil-lion pounds in Woolworths. (When I get back to London, I discover it is owned by a lottery-winning DJ from Birmingham, which seems to make perfect sense.)

I spent four months converting my CDs to MP3s (or, rather, the Apple equivalent, AAC files, which are fundamentally MP4s), and by the middle of May I had begun ripping my vinyl too. One night I'd been judging some student fashion awards in a tent in Battersea Park, and one of the organizers told me about a piece of gear called an iMic that allows you to record directly from vinyl into iTunes. This felt like the most serendipitous thing ever, and the next day I made my way to the hi-fi department in John Lewis in Oxford Street (which is where I had been told, in no uncertain terms, to go), and spent thirty-nine pounds on my Griffin iMic.

And boy did it make me happy. The first recordings I remember making were when I was about ten, in the front room of our house in Deal, the listless coastal town in Kent, with me using an external cassette microphone to record various Tiny Tots versions of Disney songs like "Old Yeller" and "Whistle While You Work"; this was going to be just as much fun, with hopefully better results.

I started with the singles, daunted somewhat by the thought of manually recording every song on some of my favorite LPs (especially Wire's *Pink Flag*, which, the last time I looked, had about sixty-three tracks on it). By recording singles I could make quantum dents in my record collection, a sort of cathartic housekeeping and rather pathetic self-management technique that would subconsciously encourage me to keep going (this was going to take a long, long time). I installed the software, connected all the leads, and adjusted the volume control just like I'd been doing for years when recording onto cassette or minidisc, making sure my Devo and Aztec Camera singles weren't going to bounce up into the red and get all distorted. Then I'd lower the needle onto the vinyl, and quickly click on the Record button on the iMic display, real-time recording every obscure and esoteric piece of my life that (for probably very sound reasons) hadn't found its way onto CD. You'd think that in this age of extravagantly produced boxed sets, where every raggedy castoff is collated and framed with perfect digital efficiency, that it would be possible to find this stuff loitering about in record shops (where I always imagine the likes of long-deleted Roberta Flack and Donny Hathaway LPs metaphorically kicking a ball against a garage door, waiting for someone like me to come along and buy them). Either that, or they would be available on the Internet.

But no, the only place this stuff existed was in my cupboards. And so I had to keep going: if I was seriously going to pour my whole life into my box, I had to squash it all in, and not just the bits that had been deemed acceptable for the CD generation. And so I began trawling through my record collection, uploading rare singles like Alternative TV's "Love Lies Limp," the seminal (ha ha), flexidisc given away by *Sniffin' Glue* in 1977; the Red Crayola's "Hurricane Fighter Plane" flexidisc I was given at a Pere Ubu concert in Chiselhirst Caves in 1978; Tony Osborne's "Shepherd's Song," a 1972 recording of a Dubonnet commercial; Iggy Pop's Siamese Records version of "I Got a Right" (again from 1977, and the only version of this song worth having), and many, many others. Of course the greatest thing about the iMic was its ability to import all my twelve-inch singles, records that had defined my life after dark through much of my youth, that had almost become part of my DNA but that I very rarely listened to anymore. (One such example is Nuance's "Loveride" on Island's original Fourth & Broadway label, a twelve-inch I bought on my first trip to New York in 1984, when I was twenty-three, and which I rather crassly said was so powerful it was actually "killing" people on the dance floor when I reviewed it for the *NME* on my return.)

So, come August, at least two-thirds of my life is in my Pod. There is still a fair bit of husbandry to take care of, but by and large I'm on the home straight. Or at least I think I am.

One afternoon in Ibiza, as we're all lazing by the pool, some of us working off hangovers, at least three of us working our way through Bob Woodward's *Plan of Attack*, and a couple of us attempting to do both, we start playing the iPod through the pool-side speaker system, pumping out one of many chill-out playlists I've compiled specifically for moments like this (in a fit of hubris, I have taken it upon myself to be the iPod DJ for a houseful of gold-standard, first-generation iPodaholics). But to my dismay, the quality is not quite what I expected it to be. The songs sound a bit . . . woody, a little dull, as though we are listening to them on an FM radio that isn't quite tuned in.

Bizarrely, the only songs that don't sound muddy are the ones recorded directly from vinyl; and not because music was better in those days, but because—*stupid man, why hadn't I realized?*—they've all been recorded on the default AIFF format. What this meant was that whereas all the songs recorded from CD had been uploaded via the MP3 (or rather AAC) format—i.e., compressed files—the vinyl recordings weren't compressed at all, as they were AIFF. The AIFF, or audio interchange file format, is one that has been used in the Macintosh operating system for ages. In a way, you could say that it is the Macintosh equivalent of wave files (meaning uncompressed audio data). The quality is far superior to that of MP3 but the file size is huge, and a full song in the AIFF format can take up to 30 MB or more of disk space. AAC—advanced audio coding—was designed to replace MP3 technology, which is now nearly twenty-five years old. But while the sound compression system is far more efficient and delivers better sound quality, nearly rivaling that of uncompressed CDs, the AIFF system actually *is* CD quality. Which is where I was obviously going wrong (by not using it, that is).

And then, with a cold sweat building up around my neck, like some sort of death-mask halo, I thought back to a couple of conversations I'd had six months previously. Robin, who had introduced me to the Altec Lansing speakers, and who seemed to be something of an expert in these matters long before I thought it was desirable to be so, had told me I ought to explore other importing preferences ("You see, I'm a sucker for quality," he'd said, as though he knew I was an amateur but was trying to soften the blow). While Richard, another good friend and the one person who had followed my burgeoning obsession with the iPod since its inception, had casually told me that compressed files were not the way to go (he was installing a solid-state music center in his house and was full of derision for any sort of compression). Shit. How could they both be right? Not only would I have to do something about my importing process, but I would have to do so without letting either of them know.

Should I dump all my AACs and bump up to AIFF? What this would mean is that while a song like, say, Miles Davis's "So What" (which lasts for nine minutes and twenty-four seconds) was only taking up 8.8 MB with AAC, if I were to convert it or import it as an AIFF, which is a noncompressed file, it would be taking up 95.1 MB, using more than ten times as much space (you can fit around ninety-two four-minute AIFF files on an iPod mini). So although I could fill up my 40 GB iPod with approximately ten thousand songs using AAC (which is 666.6 hours, or nearly enough music to play nonstop throughout the entire month of February without hearing the same song twice), the quality would eventually be found wanting.

Which is where AIFF comes in. Basically, it's better. If you read any of the dozens of iPod manuals that have been published in the past couple of years, you'll be told that AIFF files are only for fidelity fanatics, but that's not the case at all: to experience CD-quality sound you need AIFF files.

And so I had a dilemma. Should I carry on regardless, recording everything on AAC, and to hell with the consequences? Or should I start again using AIFF, safe in the knowledge that my collection was as good as it possibly could be? It would be no good converting my AAC files to AIFF files (which can be done with two swift movements inside the iTunes gateway), as all I'd be doing would be expanding an already compressed file, which is like magnifying an abridged book (it's still abridged, just bigger).

After several days of internal dialogue (I was too embarrassed to discuss it with anyone else), I decided to go for it. That night, as I was in the kitchen of our rented Balaeric palace, I casually mentioned to Richard that I might—just might, you understand—start filling my iPod all over again, and go back through my CD collection importing everything on AIFF instead of AAC. He was painstakingly making a caesar salad at the time, and, perhaps with a mixture of bewilderment and benevolent resignation, took a long hard pull on his beer and gave me a seriously old-fashioned look that said, implicitly, "You are a dear, dear friend, and whatever you decide to do will be okay with me, but I feel I have to point out to you right now that you should have thought of this *ages* ago, before you began all this nonsense, and that I want it to be logged that I think you are a sad, sad loser."

Which I thought was fair enough, really.

Prior to this I'd had other minor iPod disappointments, but none that were insurmountable. When I started listening to my iPod through headphones (something I've never been a huge fan of, preferring to listen to the iPod through speakers), I began to worry that I was going prematurely deaf, as the machine wasn't loud enough, although I soon realized this was because the European models are much quieter than their American counterparts. Some European countries—and principally I mean France—are so concerned about the dangerous mix of excessive volume and unprotected eardrums that they've barred personal listening devices such as the iPod from being louder than 100 decibels. The American iPod can play up to a theoretical limit of 104 dB, which is 2.5 times louder than 100 dB. (There are various ways to accelerate the onslaught of tinnitus, although one of the easiest is Hans-Peter Dusel's iPod VolumeBooster utility, which can be found at www.volumebooster.tangerine-soft.de/index.shtml. You could also invest in a pair of Etymotic Research's ER•6 Isolator headphones, which will cut out most extraneous outside noise. Failing that, you could start listening to Queens of the Stone Age. All of the time.)

My second problem involved my PowerBook's capacity, which after a few months I discovered wasn't as big as I'd thought it was—only 37 GB, making it impossible for me to fill my 40 GB iPod. I felt slightly conned when I found this out, as though the IT guys who'd sold me the laptop knew I was about to painstakingly import ten thousand songs onto iTunes and be unable to do anything else because my hard disk wasn't big enough. But I simply increased the memory (to 55 GB) and got on with it. After all, if I was intent on building a compact version of the Virgin Megastore, it was hardly surprising if I had to build the odd extension or two.

But having discovered my importing gaff, I vowed to go back in again, resigned myself to uploading everything I had already uploaded, but in a different, better format. Sure, at least a fifth of my iTunes collection had been transferred by AIFF from vinyl, but that still left over four thousand songs to be recorded—or rerecorded—again. Four thousand songs, roughly four hundred LP-length CDs, at roughly five minutes a pop (the time it takes to upload), meant another thirty-three hours in front of my PowerBook. Not only bearable, I reasoned, but potentially quite fun. Gore Vidal once said that the only danger in watching pornography is that it might make you want to watch *more* pornography, and I must admit the addictive nature of uploading meant that the thought of spending a day and half (nonstop, you realize), doing something I had already done before—doing lots of things I had already done before—was actually rather exciting. Sexy, even.

Consequently, I started making more lists—more considered this time—of the stuff I needed to upload, started itemizing my Steely Dan and Stevie Wonder CDs, and working out exactly how quickly I could work my way through the piles of CDs that I knew only contained one or two songs I wanted. . . . And so I decided to go back in, back into the swatches of Sinatra, the acres of Moloko, the forests of Free Design. Far from dreading the task, I was excited—editing, deleting songs not deemed essential, reducing my musical sauce even more.

But just as I was "about to go back in"—like the tagline

from yet another *Alien* or *Jaws* sequel—I stumbled across another format altogether, Apple Lossless. I had worked out that to convert my entire iTunes library to AIFF I would have to whittle down my collection, and slice off even more songs from my past. Did I really need all those Van Morrison songs? Could I live without all that Bob Dylan stuff I'd ripped basically because I thought I ought to (I only really like *Blonde on Blonde* and *Blood on the Tracks*, so why don't I leave it at that?)? And did I really need the first Blondie album? It would take me back to 1977 whenever I played it, obviously, but honestly, did I really like it, would I appreciate any of its songs cropping up unannounced in the middle of a dinner party? And what the hell was I doing with the Keane album? It had three good songs on it for Chrissakes, so why did I need it all?

And as I was mentally working my way through all of this stuff, a colleague suggested I investigate Apple Lossless, which is another way of importing your music at high quality, but without using so much space.

Jesus, I thought to myself, what now?! Would I still be rerecording this stuff when I was in my fifties? But this turned out to be the best iTip yet. In the past, if you were an audiophile and weren't concerned about the amount of space your music files consumed, you would have chosen either the WAV or, more likely, the AIFF encoder because of the resulting files' purity. But Lossless, which is a relatively new codec, offers almost exactly the same quality files as AIFF at roughly half the size. Meaning that Miles Davis's "So What," which in the AIFF format eats up a massive 95.1 MB, with Lossless comes in at a much more reasonable 55.5 MB. (Regardless of the format you choose, changing encoders and bit rates requires a trip to iTunes' Import preference pane—select Preferences from the iTunes menu in Mac OS X. Within this window you'll find iTunes' five encoding options in the Import Using pop-up menu, and when you select an encoder, its default setting will appear there. Choose AAC, for example, and you'll find that iTunes will encode a file at 128 Kbps, while MP3 files are encoded at 160 Kbps by default, even though the quality is less good.)

Armed with this knowledge, I started again; slightly irritated by the thought of repetition, but also quite fired up by it too—excited by the thought of once more hitting the air snare at the start of "Like a Rolling Stone," excited by the thought of ripping the best bits of Blur's *The Great Escape* without having to play the whole thing again, excited by the thought of importing those 112 Van Morrison songs in their entirety.

A few weeks after my conversion to Lossless I saw an ad on the Internet: "IBIZA HOUSE FOR RENT: Gingerbread style, 12 bedrooms, gym, Jacuzzi, petting zoo, indoor ice rink, popular with adult film makers." I decided to book it for next year.

15

Journey to the Center of the iPod

At last I am replete, at one with my machine

The PowerBook is sitting on the desk in my den, where it's been, by and large, for the past ten months. It sits, Zen-like, right in the middle, surrounded by my detritus, my . . . stuff. The KEF speakers still sit proudly behind it, as do the Sony twin-deck, the Audio-Technica turntable, and the mammoth Kenwood tuner. Underneath the plasma on the far wall sits my almost-installed Japanese Eclipse iPod speakers, their wires still hanging over the edge of the cabinet like ivy. There are piles of CDs, piles of magazines, piles of newspaper clippings, piles of . . . piles.

My left index finger presses the Apple key on the Power-Book as the right one presses "s," for Save. And as I do, the laptop goes "ping!" in perfect C major, the happiest chord in the world, the I-love-everybody chord. Apple put this here for a reason, to make us all feel good about using its products, and it works. This "ping!" isn't a D minor seventh, not the I'm-so-sad-I-can't-even-find-a-hooker blues chord, but the "ping!" of eternal sunshine. Sure, it also sounds like it should herald the arrival of a filtered disco record, but is that such a bad thing?

"Ping!"

And so, finally, I have finished. I have collected every single piece of good music I own in one place. Every song I have ever liked has been uploaded onto my iTunes library and transferred to my iPod. My box of memories is full, fit to bursting. Every day, every week, every month of my life is represented here in one way or another—whether it's the night I lost my virginity, or the day I fell in love with my wife. Everything has its soundtrack, and that soundtrack is on my iPod. Can this be it? Is that all there is?

The term "Elvis year" is used to describe the year of something's peak popularity (2003, for instance, was the Atkins diet's Elvis year—although which year was Elvis's Elvis year is still a matter of debate). For the iPod, so far every year since 2001 has been its Elvis year. The iPod has been such a cultural phenomenon, it has made a lot more people interested in Apple than Apple made people interested in the iPod. Millions of people own them, millions more talk about them in hushed tones, and the fusillade of third-party gadgets has contributed to an extraordinarily lush and prosperous ecosystem. There is a veritable iPodNation out there, and it is now such an intrinsic part of the pop-cultural lexicon that "i" references crop up everywhere. Take these examples from the *Future Dictionary of America*:

iGod [ay-god] *n*. a portable device (typically of 500-yottabyte capacity) that simulates the wisdom and/or awe-inspiring terror of an omnipotent deity. e.g. "I downloaded Buddhism onto my iGod last week and I've already reached a state of nirvana."

iJob [ay-job] *n*. optical liposuction for people with unfashionable fat eyes, popular in the 2010s. The

extracted material made an excellent teething gel for
babies.

The iPod became so ubiquitous that Duke University in
North Carolina started offering downloadable courses . . .
asking people what was on their iPod became an acceptable
question in job interviews . . . and in a move-on from seventies "key" parties, people in my neighborhood began throwing iPod parties, where they placed their machines in a big
bowl on the coffee table and then chose one at random to
take home (imagine the horror of taking your little digital
box of joy out to the car in the hope of pushing the sonic en-
velope only to discover it contained the complete works of
Courtney Love or the Manic Street Preachers!).

And what ructions it has caused! The music industry is in
such a state of flux that it seems unlikely to find a workable
business model that resembles any it has employed during
the past fifty years. The success of the iPod and digital downloading has affected the industry in so many different ways.

Since the beginning of the decade, magazines and newspapers have made a habit of cover-mounting CDs in the
hope of generating sales. In November 2004 *Wired* magazine
gave away a CD with a difference. All the songs came with a
license that gave anyone the permission to do more than just
listen to them. You could swap them, sample them, whatever. And most of the artists involved—Danger Mouse,
Gilberto Gil, the Thievery Corporation, David Byrne, Paul
Westerberg, etc.—went a step further and released their
songs under the more expansive Sampling Plus license,
meaning their music could be used by other people for commercial gain. Figuring the music industry is waging an un-

winnable war against technology, *Wired* decided to set a precedent and put all this stuff . . . out there.

There is also a fast-growing band of so-called podcasters—mostly amateur program-makers whose music radio shows are designed to be heard on MP3 players. Since September 2004, when new software called iPodder allowed listeners to download their favorite shows automatically, hundreds of advertisement-free radio channels have emerged in cyberspace. You just download the software at iPodder.org and decide which audio feeds to subscribe to, which are then stored on your iPod next time you sync with your laptop.

I myself have become a third-party extension, and, since loading my machine, have become something of an iPod bitch, encouraging people to send me their brand-new machines so I can put my own memories on them. A newspaper editor, a shoe designer, a singer, an architect, a literary agent, the European head of a major fashion company, a solicitor or two . . . all of them are now walking around with my memories bouncing around inside their heads. Am I helping them, or are they helping me? I wonder—am I simply saving them an awful lot of time and trouble, or am I indulging myself by foisting my taste upon them?

Ironically, especially as the iPod could turn out to be Apple's greatest success story, it was Jonathan Ive's and Steve Jobs's passion for music that helped push the product through in the first place. Yes, Jobs knew the company needed an MP3 player, and yes, like all Apple creations it was driven by commerce, but the iPod's soul, its core, is a testament to its creators' belief that music is as capable of defining today's culture as it so obviously did twenty, thirty, forty years ago. Pop's continued relevance, both to consumers and to the industry that feeds them, relies upon constant, perpetual reinvention: every eighteen months or so there needs to be a collective Damascene conversion in order to keep the whole thing fresh, the sort of groundswell that automatically makes whatever came immediately before it seem arcane and unfathomable. And in its way, the iPod is the first music carrier, and digital music technology the first delivery system, to affect the music industry in the same way as music itself.

As I reached what I thought was the end of my digital tunnel, an interested party posed two very salient questions:

1) Having compiled all this . . . stuff. What are you missing? What do you realize you need? Will you ever need any Sham 69?

2) How are you going to remember where all this stuff is?

Well, the answer to the first question is easy: everything . . . potentially. As every song on the iPod has the ability to challenge the assumptions of the one before, who knows what weird juxtaposition might work? Who's to say that there aren't a few buried gems on the many albums produced by Prince in the nineties? Who's to say that Mötley Crüe are beyond redemption? Just how many Grateful Dead albums are there out there? They can't all be bad, can they? (However there might not be any room for Sham 69, admittedly.)

And as for question two: with ease. The iPod's propulsion makes everything easy to access, while keeping that very same "everything" buried inside a labyrinth of interweaving algorithms (listen long enough and you might hear something you've never heard before).

So how was I, after my journey? Had I really captured the soul of this new machine? Or were my expectations simply resentment under construction? William Burroughs once said that we cut up the past to find the future, which, in a way, is exactly what the iPod has done, scrambling our back pages in order to create a bright new tomorrow. I certainly felt that my past had been well and truly trawled over, while I was simultaneously looking forward with a heightened sense of anticipation.

More important, was my journey actually over? Had my express train finally reached Digitopia? Far from it. No, I thought, this is only the beginning. Everything I do for the rest of my life can now be accompanied by my little white memory box. When my collection was finally all in one place I began to think of it as an arc that has followed my life, from left to right in a descending curve that eventually falls out of peripheral vision, in the bottom right-hand corner of my sightline, around the time I am 110 (by which time, no matter what Jonathan Ive designs, I shall surely be dead). Starting at the age of eight or nine with my parents' Frank Sinatra and Beatles records, my graph line then drops down to my teens and Bowie and Roxy and Alice Cooper, then runs along the straight with the arrival of punk, new romantics, antediluvian disco, clubland, and shiny eighties pop, toward a retrenchment leading to enlightenment (i.e., when I started listening to my old records again). As the curve starts racing toward my thirties, I think of Van Morrison and Bruce Springsteen, and a pre-midlife curiosity for things I had previously ignored or missed. And then, just as my arc had begun tailing off . . . up pops the iPod icon, just like it does on my PowerBook. There it is! The UberPod, standing proud and tall, a black hole full of everything from my past, everything from my present, and as much from my future as I've got time for.

Crucially, it began dawning on me that my journey had been a destination in itself. John Lennon liked to say that life is what happens when you're busy making other plans (he even said it in song once), and my iPod journey is testament to that.[9] I have learned so much about music, about myself, during the time I've been "at one" with my machine—the results of which are included here, deep in these pages—that I've begun to think that my hobby is a vocation after all, and that what I always thought was a parallel universe is in fact my own private universe, of which there is only one.

What I know for a fact is that this is the first time I can remember technology influencing content, or the consumption of content, in such a profound way. The iPod has totally rejuvenated my interest in music, and over my nine-month induction period I became a man obsessed, buying dozens and dozens of new CDs, dozens and dozens of old CDs I thought I'd never get round to listening to, and borrowing, burning, and downloading like a crazy person. The iPod reminded me that music is compelling, all-consuming, and

[9] Spending thirty years collecting the various bits and pieces required to build a decent version of the Beach Boys' *Smile* seemed like an honorable task, and one that has occupied an inordinate amount of my time, but having got there, having achieved my goal, when Brian Wilson finally released his rerecorded interpretation in 2004, all I felt was a massive sense of deflation. It was all right, I thought to myself, but *(a)* it's not quite as good, *(b)* now everyone's got it, and *(c)* what do I do now?

continually diverting. And, right now, the more I hear, the more I want. John Peel, who was perhaps the greatest and most vocal supporter of "new" music—or at the very least a man who spent more time listening to music than probably anyone else has ever done—had this to say about his continual quest for the new:

> There's always the possibility that you're going to come across a record that transforms your life. And it happens weekly. It's like a leaf on the stream. There are little currents and eddies and sticks lying in the water that nudge you in a slightly different direction. And then you break loose and carry on down the current. There's nothing that actually stops you and lifts you out of the water and puts you on the bank but there are diversions and distractions and alarums and excursions, which is what makes life interesting really. Not in a Roman Emperor kind of way where you have an *excess* of stimulation—I forget which Emperor it was that used to have animal skins thrown over him and then scamper into an arena and claw testicles off naked slaves with his bare hands, not quite *that* level—but a little excitement here and there. And music provides that. It's fantastic.

Without the iPod it's unlikely I would have bought Rilo Kiley's astonishing CD *The Execution of All Things,* nor bothered to buy the early work of Stephen Stills, stuff that I always thought I might like but had never cared enough about to find out (it's not bad). And the way I feel about music now is a bit like that: I don't want to miss anything, don't want to miss the next Strokes record, wouldn't want to miss the new Coldplay CD, couldn't bear to miss Steely Dan's "future project," can't wait to hear the new U2 (and there's always a new U2). Patti Smith once said, in the way she once said things (about 1975, I reckon, at the time of *Horses*), that the only reason she hadn't committed suicide was because she'd miss the next Stones album, and while I am about as far from committing suicide as a person can be, and while I have almost no desire to hear the next Stones album (and I'm fairly sure I wasn't that bothered in 1975, actually), I sort of see what she meant. Music now feels as important to me as it did at the age of twelve, sixteen, or twenty (and they were very good years—Bowie, the Ramones, Chic)—perhaps it always was, but I somehow *feel* it more now.

One of the least expected endorsements of the iPod came from the White House in April 2005, when George Bush announced he was a partial adopter. In between his return from Pope John Paul II's funeral in Rome and a meeting with Israeli Prime Minister Ariel Sharon, President Bush spent ninety minutes on an eighteen-mile mountain-bike ride at his Texas ranch, a ride on which he was apparently accompanied by his favorite exercise toy: an iPod loaded with "country," "rock," and "pop" (no doubt compiled with the aim of getting the presidential heart rate up to a chest-pounding 170 beats per minute). We don't know for sure whether Dubya compiled his iPod himself (unlikely, as some of the songs were suggested by Mark McKinnon, a biking buddy and his chief media strategist during the 2004 campaign), although this is what was on it: Van Morrison's "Brown Eyed Girl," John Fogerty's "Centerfield," "(You're So Square) Baby, I Don't Care" by Joni Mitchell, and the deeply suspect "My Sharona" by power-pop wannabes the Knack. He was given his machine by his daughters, and at the time of his bike ride it contained just 250 songs. The president's revelations prompted a splurge of guilty iPod confessions from the most unlikely celebrities, the strangest of which was undoubtedly Germaine Greer's penchant for Frank Zappa (and in particular, "Call Any Vegetable" and "G-Spot Tornado").

I was less surprised to learn that Burt Bacharach owns one. When I interviewed the seventy-seven-year-old composer three months before this book was published, up in his palatial Pacific Palisades dream home in L.A.—the sort of house I might have envisaged him living in during the 1960s, with all the prerequisites of future-retro suburbia, including a bachelor den, a music room, pool house, barbeque patio, and open-plan kitchen—he eulogized the little white box. It was uploaded for him by his twelve-year-old son, Oliver, who filled it with his father's favorites, notably James Ingram and old Motown. Bacharach never listens to his own records, at least his old ones ("Why should I? I know it all"), and if he listens to anything at all it's stuff he's working on at the moment. When we met he was working on an orchestral concept album with Dr. Dre and Rufus Wainwright, and it sounded great, a lush and convoluted symphony that evoked all those common epiphanies of yesteryear.

And as for Steve Jobs and Apple? As the competition fails to come up with a credible "iPodKiller," it appears their hegemony will continue until the idea of a machine that stores 15,000, 25,000, 50,000 songs seems—God forbid—old fashioned or unnecessary. In October 2004 Steve Jobs announced the launch of the iPod Photo, a 60 GB iPod, capable of storing up to 15,000 songs as well as 25,000 wallet-sized full-color digital images. At the San Jose launch, Jobs described how he could now create slide shows to accompany his music selections, as well as album covers, and started repeating the mantra "all of your songs and photos in your pocket." Amazingly, the new iPod could do all this and was just one millimeter thicker than the G4. This was a remarkable feat of engineering, and immediately made me stop worrying about whether or not I'd be able to fit everything I own onto my 40 GB (all I had to do was upgrade).

Its launch was also indicative of the iPod's future—it's exponential, and will soon no doubt be able to suck everything into its shiny white casing. This prompts me to ask myself whether or not I want a machine that acts as a mobile phone–video streaming–personal organizer–type thing that allows me to send and receive e-mails while I watch *Taxi Driver*, write a column for *GQ*, and look at my holiday snaps at the same time. But soon I may have no choice. By then Apple will have no doubt effectively turned into a record company, signing bands and releasing their stuff exclusively via iTunes. Who knows? In a short while it's quite conceivable that as we enter the age of the end of ownership, we'll be able to instantly download any song we like (i.e., every song that's ever been recorded anywhere by anyone) onto our mobile phone, while the whole notion of actually bothering to curate music ourselves will seem quaint and ridiculously time-consuming. Maybe the iPod could become totally cognitive, and anticipate mood through a mixture of logic and intuition.

The future looks limitless: nowadays it doesn't seem so fanciful to suppose that if, say, in a few years we want to imagine what it would sound like for Babyshambles (if Pete Doherty isn't dead by then) to record the Rolling Stones' *Aftermath* in its entirety, because of the sophisticated wizardry of digital manipulation, this would be entirely possible (just imagine, with your new Microsoft iPod Expo-Remix all you need do is press the Create button, then "Babyshambles" then "*Aftermath*," then "All," then "Imagine," and in less time than it took you to come up with the idea in the first place, there it would be, playing in your home, your car, in the homes and cars of everyone you know, or, maybe, simply playing in your head, where you'll indulge it for a few minutes before asking your machine to get Pink Floyd to cover the complete works of Orbital (just imagine . . .).

More prosaically, it will soon be possible for any domestic music player to take remix culture as far as anyone could possibly want it to: if you want to remix "Blue Monday" so it lasts three hours, then why not? If your perverted sense of the zeitgeist determines that you fancy listening to a calypso remix of "Smells Like Teen Spirit" then who's to deny you? No one.

But you might just enjoy the thought of playing the first track of every Beatles album as you drive to work tomorrow morning—and with digital potential, you'll be able to configure this on your music carrier in the time it takes you to find your car keys (and in my case, probably less time). Your machine will soon be able to download directly from any online music store, as well as being able to tune in to every radio program that has been broadcast in living memory.

Or, you just might want to wallow in a day's worth of Joni Mitchell—scramble the stuff up, tell your machine to try and anticipate your Saturday morning mood (with specially designated pauses for eating, peeing, and reading the newspapers), and then just play away.

Which is just what I'm doing now, playing away, letting my machine whisk me away and sweep me through the farthermost reaches of my mind, taking me through my past, my present, and, by dint of random juxtaposition, my future too. Right now I am exerting complete control, keeping a tight hand on the tiller. For while the world of abundance is as appealing as any Shangri-La, I know that for me personally, individuality will be the key to any successful navigation.

In the course of the next half an hour I will listen to a song I first enjoyed at the age of eight (the Rushmorean "Hey Jude"); a song I've only heard once before in my life ("Willow Weep for Me" from Dexter Gordon's *Our Man in Paris*); two Johnny Cash tracks; and a song that means as much to me now as it did when I first heard it, a song that means so much to me it has the capacity to occasionally make me well up. That song is "Being Boring" by the Pet Shop Boys (6.50 minutes from *Behaviour*, Parlophone, October 1990, the melancholic classic written by Neil Tennant and Chris Lowe), and the salient lyrics are these: "Now I sit with different faces / In rented rooms and foreign places / All the people I was kissing / Some are here and some are missing / In the nineteen nineties / I never dreamt that I would get to be / The creature that I always meant to be / But I thought in spite of dreams / You'd be sitting somewhere here with me . . . "

Well, while some people might not be with me now, the records we listened to together are all here in my little white memory box, all lovingly compiled and curated, just waiting for that time when I might need them again.

And I think that time is just about now . . .

Appendix

There are those who would say that the iTunes facility is little but a glorified, animated list—a fully functional, battery-powered litany—which, I suppose, is why I like it so much. I no longer have to scour my CD shelves for the Eminem album with "Stan" on it, I don't have to shuffle around looking for a Sex Pistols single I'm not even sure I have anymore (how can you lose a picture-sleeve copy of "Pretty Vacant"?), and there's no need for me to get down on my hands and knees and inspect the curling spines of my LPs searching for the Smiths' *Hatful of Hollow* (which, I must admit, I haven't done since I was about twenty-three), or one of my rare Japanese limited-edition David Bowie albums. With my PowerBook it's just a scroll in the park.

The list has become one of the defining characteristics of our time, whether it's one of those *100 Best* programs on Channel 4 (*100 Best Wednesday Afternoon Game Shows, 100 Worst Channel 5 Programmes Starring an Ex-Member of a Partially Successful Boy Band* . . .), or the first thirty pages of any blue-collar men's magazine, or page 3 of any national broadsheet (" . . . in a massive, nationwide poll undertaken by the *Daily Telegraph* we've discovered that the country's favorite Lenny Kravitz song is 'It Ain't Over Till It's Over,' principally because that was the only one most of you could remember . . ."). Today's culture is a list culture, but then that's hardly surprising. The Internet, Satellite TV, DVDs, the constant repackaging, and reorganizing of old pop music (we live, in case you hadn't realized, in a compilation culture that threatens to disappear up its own fundament), the revisionist and often reductive nature of music magazines, the fact that fifty years of pop culture are now available as soon as you press the Return button on your keyboard . . . it's all conspired to turn the past into the present, and the future into the past.

Everything is there if we want it, which, it has to be said, we do. I do, anyway. iTunes has condoned my obsessive, nerdlike tendencies, outed me as a collector, a hoarder, an adolescent (though not so adolescent anymore) list maker. And boy have I leaped at the opportunity: B-sides that are better than their A-sides, ten solo Beatles songs about being in the Beatles, ten genitally obsessed Red Hot Chili Peppers songs, Frank Sinatra songs he recorded while wearing a hat, songs one of my best friends thought were by the Doors but were actually by R. Dean Taylor (one: "There's a Ghost in My House"), the 350 greatest rap diss songs—ever! (How about "Takeover" by Jay-Z, which gives Mobb Deep the finger.) Songs that send shivers up your spine when the singer sings the words "Steve McQueen" (two: "Absent Friends" by the Divine Comedy and "Electrolite" by R.E.M.) Songs with either *blue* in the title ("Blue Eyes" by Elton John, "Blue Hotel" by Chris Isaak, "Blue Money" by Van Morrison), or *big* ("Big Log" by Robert Plant, "Big Louise" by Scott Walker, "Big Time" by Neil Young). The capacity for iTunes lists is exponential.

If songs really are little houses in which our hearts once lived, then surely it's our duty to build gargantuan pleasure palaces where they all can live. After all, the iPod is nothing if not a memory box.

Creating playlists on iTunes doesn't use up any more space, it just reconfigures the files in a different order, so you can make as many as you like (they're all joined by invisible umbilical c(h)ords). TV theme tunes? Download/upload them all! (For the record, the stars of Boss Cat, so-called in the U.K. because of a well-known cat food, were Top Cat, Spook, Fancy, Brain, Choo Choo, and Benny. Oh, and officer Dibble.) Britpop casualties? The playlist can be as long as you like!

After I'd collated around a dozen playlists (artist-specific: Beatles, Beach Boys, Springsteen, Steely Dan, Marvin Gaye, U2, Afrika Bambaataa, R.E.M., Coldplay, Libertines), I started to get inventive. Could I create a playlist featuring only records that had great hi-hat sounds (the best hi-hat sound ever recorded is on the O'Jays' "I Love Music")?[10] Could I create a playlist that consisted of records that sounded like they were recorded by the Rolling Stones but obviously weren't? A playlist featuring Radiohead's best

---

[10]As for the best pre-digital, analog drum sound—in case you were wondering, and I think you probably were—check out Elton John's "Someone Saved My Life Tonight" on *Captain Fantastic and the Brown Dirt Cowboy* (DJM, 1975). The drums were played by Nigel Olsson, and produced by Gus Dudgeon. I met Dudgeon once, and when I told him I thought he had recorded the best drum sound in the history of twentieth-century music, he looked at me quizzically, and said, without a hint of arrogance: "That's weird. That's the second time I've been told that this month."

songs (actually quite a few. I had an irrational and rather childish dislike of the band—spotty Oxford students, I thought, yuk—until my brother exasperatedly sat me down one night and talked, and played, me through them; so three at least: "High and Dry," "Fake Plastic Trees," and "The Bends," all from *The Bends*)? A playlist featuring piano-led songs all played in the key of E? How about an imaginary colloquial British rap concept album featuring alternating tracks by Mike Skinner and John Cooper Clarke?

After a while I realized I could do all this, and more. A lot, lot more . . .

The iPod's Greatest Hits: 100 Songs You Absolutely Must Have in Your Life

1. "Tiny Dancer" by Elton John. 2. "Scar Tissue" by Red Hot Chili Peppers. 3. "Pure Pleasure Seeker" by Moloko. 4. "School Spirit" by Kanye West. 5. "Cannonball" by Damien Rice. 6. "I Want You" by Bob Dylan. 7. "Ceremony" by New Order. 8. "Butterfly Collector" by the Jam. 9. "Babe I'm Gonna Leave You" by Led Zeppelin. 10. "It's Now or Never" by Elvis Presley. 11. "High and Dry" by Radiohead. 12. "Save the Country" by The 5th Dimension. 13. "Planet Rock" by Afrika Bambaataa. 14. "STD 0632" by Alan Hull. 15. "I Can't Stand the Rain" by Ann Peebles. 16. "Tighten Up" by Archie Bell and the Drells. 17. "A Night in Tunisia" by Art Blakey. 18. "Miss You" by the Rolling Stones. 19. "Ready for Love" by Bad Company. 20. "Rough Boy" by ZZ Top. 21. "What a Waste" by Ian Dury and the Blockheads. 22. "Theme from *Shaft*" by Isaac Hayes. 23. "The Pretender" by Jackson Browne. 24. "Magnolia" by J. J. Cale. 24. "Silly Games" by Janet Kay. 25. "Grace" by Jeff Buckley. 26. "She's

Gone" by Hall and Oates. 27. "Behind the Mask" by the Yellow Magic Orchestra. 27. "Chalkhills and Children" by XTC. 28. "Blue Red and Grey" by the Who. 29. "Dead Leaves and the Dirty Ground" by the White Stripes. 30. "Such a Night" by Dr. John. 31. "Black Water" by the Doobie Brothers. 32. "A Girl Like You" by Edwyn Collins. 33. "Indian" by Eg and Alice. 34. "Miss Otis Regrets" by Ella Fitzgerald. 35. "Big Tears" by Elvis Costello. 36. "I Found a Reason" by the Velvet Underground. 37. "Walk On" by U2. 38. "Hey Fellas" by Trouble Funk. 39. "Hidden Treasure" by Traffic. 40. "New York's a Lonely Town" by the Trade Winds. 41. "Plain Sailing" by Tracey Thorn. 42. "Broken Bicycles" by Tom Waits. 43. "I Need to Know" by Tom Petty and the Heartbreakers. 44. "Just One Victory" by Todd Rundgren. 45. "Encore" by DJ Danger Mouse. 46. "New York Minute" by Don Henley. 47. "On the Dunes" by Donald Fagen. 48. "The True Wheel" by Brian Eno. 49. "Debris" by the Faces. 50. "My Friend the Sun" by Family. 51. "The Chain" by Fleetwood Mac. 52. "Janis" by Focus. 53. "The Night" by Frankie Valli. 54. "Kites Are Fun" by the Free Design. 55. "Think It Over" by the Thorns. 56. "Private Plane" by Thomas Leer. 57. "Humph" by Thelonious Monk. 58. "Advice for the Young at Heart" by Tears For Fears. 59. "Come with Me" by Tania Maria. 60. "Don't Worry About the Government" by Talking Heads. 61. "Mr. Davies" by Tahiti 80. 62. "From My Window" by Swing Out Sister. 63. "Rudy" by Supertramp. 64. "Hoover Dam" by Sugar. 65. "The Gardener of Eden" by the Style Council. 66. "Last Night" by the Strokes. 67. "Different Drum" by the Stone Poneys. 68. "Pastime Paradise" by Stevie Wonder. 69. "Serenade" by the Steve Miller Band. 70. "Feel So Real" by Steve Arrington. 71. "Cybele's Reverie" by Stereolab. 72.

"Johnny's Garden" by Stephen Stills. **73.** "I Was Dancing in the Lesbian Bar" by Jonathan Richman. **74.** "Jump to the Beat" by Stacy Lattisaw. **75.** "Do Nothing" by the Specials. **76.** "Journey" by the Gentle People. **77.** "Give Me the Night" by George Benson. **78.** "Costa del Sol" by Gero. **79.** "Sister Sadie" by the Gil Evans Orchestra. **80.** "Beautiful" by Gordon Lightfoot. **81.** "Undun" by the Guess Who. **82.** "Wake Up Everybody" by Harold Melvin and the Blue Notes. **83.** "This Is Mine" by Heaven 17. **84.** "Little One" by Herbie Hancock. **85.** "The Girl with the Loneliest Eyes" by the House of Love. **86.** "Tiny Girls" by Iggy Pop. **87.** "A Song for Europe" by Roxy Music. **88.** "The Seed (2.0)" by the Roots. **89.** "A Laugh for Rory" by Rahsaan Roland Kirk. **90.** "Gradually Learning" by the Rockingbirds. **91.** "The Fool" by Robert Gordon. **92.** "Me and My Monkey" by Robbie Williams. **93.** "Scattered" by Ray Davies. **94.** "Jive Samba" by Quincy Jones. **95.** "Babies" by Pulp. **96.** "Prototype" by OutKast. **97.** "Loveride" by Nuance. **98.** "Lotus" by R.E.M. **99.** "Starfish and Coffee" by Prince. **100.** "Vanilla Sky" by Paul McCartney.

Acknowledgments

I'd like to thank my employers at Condé Nast, Nicholas Coleridge and Jonathan Newhouse, for all their help and encouragement, my brilliant agent, Ed Victor (who got the idea immediately), Alan Samson (who bought it), Daniel Walter (who originally suggested it), Mel Agace, Richard Campbell-Breeden, Tony Parsons, Oliver Peyton, Stuart Morgan, Robin Derrick, Bill Prince, Julian Alexander, Andrew Hale, Debra Bourne, Camilla McPhie, Andy Morris, Daniel Jones, Danielle (for the typing), Edie and Georgia (for continually asking "Is Daddy iPodding again?"), and my wife, Sarah, the iPod widow, who essentially told me to get on with it.

A Note on the Author

Dylan Jones is the editor in chief of British *GQ*. A four-time Magazine Editor of the Year award winner, he was formerly the editor of *Arena* and *i-D*. He has also been an editor at the *Face*, the *Sunday Times*, and the *Observer*. His previous book, *Jim Morrison: Dark Star*, was a *New York Times* bestseller.

A Note on the Type

The text of this book is set in Linotype Sabon, named after the type founder, Jacques Sabon. It was designed by Jan Tschichold and jointly developed by Linotype, Monotype, and Stempel, in response to a need for a typeface to be available in identical form for mechanical hot metal composition and hand composition using foundry type.

Tschichold based his design for Sabon roman on a font engraved by Garamond, and Sabon italic on a font by Granjon. It was first used in 1966 and has proved an enduring modern classic.